Cantonese
Culture
and Society

广东文化与社会

刘 程　Liu Cheng　编
杨苏安　Yang Su'an　译

华南理工大学出版社
SOUTH CHINA UNIVERSITY OF TECHNOLOGY PRESS
·广州·

图书在版编目（CIP）数据

广东文化与社会：汉英对照 / 刘程编；杨苏安译. —广州：华南理工大学出版社，2017.11（2024.1重印）
Cantonese Culture and Society
ISBN 978-7-5623-4464-3

Ⅰ.①广… Ⅱ.①刘… ②杨… Ⅲ.①汉语–对外汉语教学–语言读物 ②地方文化–介绍–广东省–汉、英 Ⅳ.① H195.5 ② G127.65

中国版本图书馆 CIP 数据核字（2014）第 260809 号

广东文化与社会

刘　程　Liu Cheng　　编　　杨苏安　Yang Su'an　　译

出 版 人：柯 宁
出版发行：华南理工大学出版社
　　　　　（广州五山华南理工大学 17 号楼，邮编 510640）
　　　　　http://hg.cb.scut.edu.cn　　E-mail: scutc13@scut.edu.cn
　　　　　营销部电话：020-87113487　87111048（传真）
策划编辑：吴翠微
责任编辑：吴翠微
印 刷 者：广州小明数码印刷有限公司
开　　本：787mm×960mm　1/32　印张：8.125　字数：306千
版　　次：2017年11月第1版　2024年1月第2次印刷
定　　价：30.00元

版权所有　盗版必究　　印装差错　负责调换

前 言
Foreword

《广东文化与社会》是供海外汉语学习者使用的普及型、口语化的文化辅助读物,同时可供对广东文化感兴趣的人士阅读。

随着"汉语热"在世界范围内的持续升温和中国文化"走出去"步伐的进一步加快,海外汉语学习者和对广东文化感兴趣的人士的数量也在不断增长。作为中国文化板块中独具地域特色和侨乡色彩的广东文化,也需要紧跟时代步伐,为中国文化"走出去"及其与世界其他文化的沟通、交流、融合助力。世界范围内文化交流与融合的大潮席卷而来,《广东文化与社会》正是这一浪潮中的一朵小花。

本读本全面介绍广东文化,包括广东文化的构成、广东文化的特点、广东人、广东人的生活、主要城市、传统艺术、名胜古迹、建筑、工艺美术、民俗、风景名胜、文化名人、经济。其中"广东文化的构成""广东文化的特点""广东人"这三部分是总括部分,起提纲挈领的作用,给读者广东文化一个的总体印象,建议读者先阅读这三个部分,其他部分可不按照先

前言

This book, *Guangdong Culture and Society*, is a general reading material for those abroad who wish to learn more about China's history and language and also for people who are specifically interested in Guangdong culture.

As more and more people worldwide are keen to learn Chinese language and culture, a great number of people are becoming more interested in Guangdong culture as well. Guangdong Province has unique geographical features and is full of special characteristics of overseas Chinese and it also needs to keep up with the pace of the mainstream trend of time including worldwide cultural exchanges and integration from Chinese culture. Among this are great tides of worldwide culture exchanges and communication, *Guangdong Culture and Society* is a wave.

This book is a comprehensive introduction to Guangdong, including the compositions and characteristics of Guangdong culture, people in Guangdong and their daily life. Among this information are the major cities, traditional arts, historical sites, architectures, arts and crafts, folklore, scenic resorts, celebrities, economic development, and much more. The chapters on "Compositions of Guangdong Culture", "Characteristics of Guangdong Culture" and "People in Guangdong" are general and basic introductions and give the readers an overall impression about Guangdong culture and should be read first. The other chapters can be read in random order.

前言
Foreword

后顺序阅读。

本读本选材以能够代表广东文化为标准，突出广东文化的地域特点，或在历史上有重大影响，或至今仍影响着广东文化，不猎奇、不迎合；不止介绍古代广东文化，当代广东文化也一并纳入。读本充分考虑到海外读者的文化背景和阅读习惯，行文言简意赅，评价公正准确。

由于时间所限，书中错漏或不当之处在所难免，欢迎读者提出宝贵意见，以便修订。

刘 程
于广州大学城
2014年10月20日

The topics chosen in this book are meant to be standardized as signs of Guangdong culture, highlighting the geographical features of Guangdong culture, or having a significant impact on history, and points which still affect Guangdong culture. Not a mere novelty, nor favoritism, this book is a combined introduction to both ancient Guangdong culture and contemporary culture with consideration of the reading habits among overseas Chinese, with concise language, as well as a fair and accurate evaluation.

Due to time constraints, errors, omissions, or irregularities are inevitable and any advices are welcomed so that we can make the necessary amendments later.

目 录
Contents

1 广东文化的构成 Compositions of Guangdong Culture / 001

2 广东文化的特点 Characteristics of Guangdong Culture / 007

3 广东人 People in Guangdong / 013

广东三大民系 Three Main Ethnic Groups / 014
农民工 Migrant Workers / 018
广东老外 Foreigners in Guangdong / 022

4 广东人的生活 People's Daily Life in Guangdong / 025

凉茶 Herbal Tea / 026
靓汤 Soup / 028
糖水 Sweet Soup / 030
早茶 Morning Tea / 032
粤菜 Cantonese Cuisine / 036
粤语 Yue Dialect / 038

5 广东主要城市 Major Cities in Guangdong / 041

广州 Guangzhou / 042
深圳 Shenzhen / 044
珠海 Zhuhai / 048
中山 Zhongshan / 052
东莞 Dongguan / 054

6 广东传统艺术 Guangdong Traditional Arts / 059

采茶戏 Tea-picking Opera / 060
广东音乐 Guangdong Music / 062
客家山歌 Hakka Hill Songs / 064
岭南画派 Lingnan School of Painting / 066
木偶戏 Puppet Show / 070
粤剧 Yue Opera / 072

7 广东名胜古迹 Guangdong Historical Sites / 075

陈家祠 Chen Clan Temple / 076
南海神庙 Temple of Nanhai God / 080
南海一号 Sunken Vessel Nanhai No.1 / 084
南华禅寺 Nanhua Temple / 088
南越王墓 Nanyue King Tomb / 092
七星岩摩崖石刻 Qixingyan Moya Stone Carvings / 096
镇海楼 Zhenhai Tower / 100

8 广东建筑 Guangdong Architectures / 103

广东园林 Guangdong Gardens / 104
广州塔 Canton Tower / 110
怀圣寺 Huaisheng Mosque / 112
开平碉楼 Kaiping Diaolous / 116
骑楼 Riding Buildings / 120
圣心大教堂 Sacred Heart Cathedral / 124
围龙屋 Round-dragon Houses / 128
西关大屋 Xiguan Houses / 132
中山纪念堂 Sun Yat-sen Memorial Hall / 136

9 广东工艺美术 Guangdong Arts and Crafts / 141

端砚 Duan Inkstones / 142
佛山木版年画 Foshan Woodblock New Year Pictures / 144
广彩 Cantonese Porcelain / 146
广式家具 Cantonese Furniture / 148

广绣 Cantonese Embroidery / 150
广州盆景 Cantonese Bonsai / 154
雷州石狗 Leizhou Stone Dog Sculptures / 156
木雕 Wood-carvings / 158
瓶内画 Inner Painting / 160
吴川泥塑 Wuchuan Clay Sculptures / 164
阳江风筝 Yangjiang Kites / 166

10 广东民俗 Guangdong Folk Traditions / 171

"意头" "Yi Tou" / 172
工夫茶 KungFu Tea / 174
花市 Flower Markets / 176
菊花会 Chrysanthemum Fairs / 178
荔枝节 Lychee Festivals / 180
龙舟赛 Dragon Boat Racing / 182
皮影戏 Pi Ying Play / 186
醒狮 Lion Dance / 188

11 广东风景名胜 Guangdong Scenic Resorts / 191

白云山 Baiyun Mountain / 192
丹霞山 Danxia Mountain / 194
鼎湖山 Dinghu Mountain / 196
黄埔军校 Whampoa Military Academy / 198
李小龙乐园 Bruce Lee Theme Park / 202
罗浮山 Luofu Mountain / 204
西樵山 Xiqiao Mountain / 208

12 广东文化名人 Guangdong Celebrities / 213

陈献章 Chen Xianzhang / 214
红线女 Hung Sin-nui / 216
惠能 Hui Neng / 218
康有为 Kang Youwei / 222
李嘉诚 Li Ka-shing / 226
李小龙 Bruce Lee / 228

孙中山 Sun Yat-sen　/ 232
冼星海 Xian Xinghai　/ 236

13 广东经济 Guangdong Economy　/ 239

海上丝绸之路 Maritime Silk Road　/ 240
改革开放 Reform and Opening-up　/ 242
世界工厂 World's Factory　/ 246
广交会 Canton Fair　/ 248

1 广东文化的构成
Compositions of Guangdong Culture

广东文化包括本土文化、南迁的中原[①]文化、海洋文化和侨乡文化。

广东地处亚热带的五岭[②]之南,广东的土著是古百越族先民。广东依山傍海,河流众多,从早期的渔猎文明,到后来的农业文明,再到现代的商业文明,都表现出和中原文化不一样的特点,即喜流动、不保守。这是广东的本土文化。

秦汉以后,中国统一,广东和中原的交流日益密切。因驻军、贬官、移民的南迁,中原文化影响到广东,构成广东文化的主体。这是南迁到广东的中原文化。

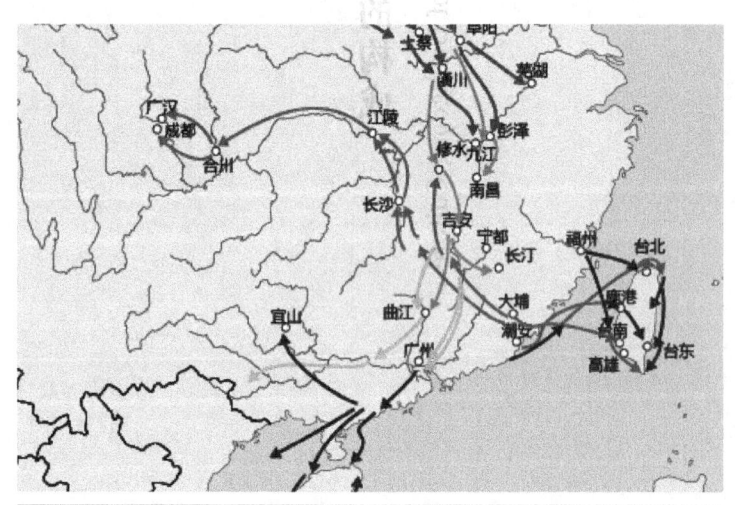

---

①中原指以洛阳、开封、商丘、安阳、郑州、南阳为中心,包括黄河中下游一带的广大平原地区。

②五岭,又叫南岭,指横亘在江西、湖南、广东、广西之间的大庾岭、骑田岭、都庞岭、萌渚岭、越城岭。

1 广东文化的构成
Compositions of Guangdong Culture

Guangdong culture is a mix of traditions from the local dwellers, Central China [1] immigrants, maritime Chinese, and residents in overseas Chinese homeland.

Guangdong Province is located on the southern side of the Wuling Mountain Range [2] and the indigenous people were known as Baiyue tribes in ancient times. There are large areas of mountains, long sea coast lines and numerous rivers in Guangdong Province. From ancient fishing and hunting civilisation, early agriculture civilisation to the current modern commercialised society, this ever changing and non-conservative culture has many very unique characteristics, compared with that of Central China. This is Guangdong local culture.

China was unified after the Qin and Han Dynasties and as a result communications between Guangdong and Central China have become more and more frequent. Guangdong culture was significantly influenced by Central China's culture by way of many troops, officials, and immigrants from Central China. The adopted Central China culture then became the main stream of the Guangdong culture.

---

[1] Central China covers the area of the vast plains along the middle and lower reaches of the Yellow River, around cities of Luoyang, Kaifeng, Shangqiu, Anyang, Zhengzhou and Nanyang.

[2] Wuling Mountain Range, also called Nanling, are five mountain ranges that lie between Jiangxi, Hunan, Guangdong, Guangxi Provinces, which namely are Dayuling Mountain, Qitianling Mountain, Dupangling Mountain, Mengzhuling Mountain and Yuechengling Mountain.

作为海上丝绸之路的起点和通商港口,广东一直是中西文化交流的平台,外来文化给广东文化带来活力。同时,中国的商品和文化也通过广东走向世界。近代,广东向西方学习先进的科学和民主思想,成为中国民主革命的发源地,在中国的民主化进程中发挥了巨大的作用。这是广东的海洋文化。

江门市是中国第一侨乡,是华侨文化的发祥地之一。祖籍江门的华侨、华人和港澳台同胞达400多万人,分布在世界上的100多个国家和地区。华侨华人在江门市的开平市留下了中西合璧的碉楼建筑。改革开放①以来,侨资企业带来先进的技术和管理理念,全市现有侨资企业超过2300家,投资总额100多亿美元,从业人员达20多万。这是广东的侨乡文化。

①改革开放是20世纪70年代末中国开始实行的改革经济、对外开放的政策。改革经济首先是从农村开始的。

1 广东文化的构成
Compositions of Guangdong Culture

As the important commercial port and the origin of the so called Maritime Silk Road, Guangdong has been acting as the communication platform between the West and China. It was foreign cultures that brought new energy into Guangdong, at the same time Chinese commodities and culture also spread to other parts of the world. In modern times, Guangdong absorbed advanced science and technology and democratic ideologies, which evolved into the origin of the Chinese Democracy Revolution and greatly contributed to Chinese democratic development. This is the maritime culture in Guangdong.

Jiangmen City is the number one immigrant homeland in China and it is one of the origins of the overseas Chinese homeland culture. Overseas Chinese from Jiangmen, with compatriots from Taiwan, Hong Kong and Macao now have exceeded 4 million in population and they spread to more than 100 countries and areas around the world. The Western-Chinese style tower architecture (Diāolóu) in Kaiping, Jiangmen City, built by the overseas Chinese is just one of many good examples. Since Reform and Opening-up Policy[①], private enterprises and companies invested by overseas Chinese and compatriots from Taiwan, Hong Kong and Macao have brought in advanced technologies and modern management. There are now more than 2,300 enterprises and companies of this type in Jiangmen City, and the investment in total exceeds 10 billon US dollars, and more than 200,000 people are employed. This is overseas Chinese homeland culture which Guangdong was based on.

---

① Reform and Opening-up Policy was the policy of economic reform and open-door implemented in the late 1970's in China. The economic reform began from the countryside.

2 广东文化的特点
Characteristics of Guangdong Culture

广东文化具有开放性、超越传统、实利重商的特点。

开放性

作为海上丝绸之路的起点和通商港口，广东一直是中西方文化交流的平台，广东文化具有一种与众不同的开放性。怀圣寺，圣心大教堂，南海一号古沉船，开平碉楼，继承国画传统技法、借鉴西洋画的技巧而形成的岭南画派，吸取中国其他七大菜系[①]的技艺、凝聚西方菜肴风格而形成的粤菜，由英国公司设计的广州塔，改革开放以来居住在广东的数十万的外国人，等等，都是广东文化开放性的表现。

---

①菜系是指在用料、刀工、制作等方面经过长期演变而形成的、具有鲜明地方特色、并具备一定规模体系的菜肴流派。粤菜、鲁菜、川菜、苏菜、浙菜、闽菜、湘菜、徽菜被称为中国"八大菜系"。

2 广东文化的特点
Characteristics of Guangdong Culture

The uniqueness of Guangdong culture includes "openness", "creativity" and a positive attitude towards business called "pro-business".

Openness

Guangdong is quite unique in this aspect since it is an important commercial port and the origin of the so-called Maritime Silk Road. Guangdong has been acting as the main communication platform between China and the Western world. The typical examples of Guangdong openness can be exhibited by Huaisheng Mosque, Catholic Cathedral, Sunken Vessel "Nanhai No.1", Kaiping Tower, and Lingnan School of Painting which has been inherited from traditional Chinese painting techniques together with that learned from Western painting styles. Also included in this is Cantonese cuisine which not only absorbed good culture from other Chinese Seven Major Cuisines [1], but also learned new ideas from Western cuisines and Canton Tower, designed by a British company. There are currently hundreds of thousands of foreigners living in Guangdong.

---

[1] A cuisine is a cuisine genre, in terms of selecting materials, cutting and preparing, and cooking methods, gradually formed with distinctive local characteristics and with a certain scale. Guangdong, Shandong, Sichuan, Jiangsu, Zhejiang, Fujian, Hunan, Anhui cuisines are known as China's Eight Major Cuisines.

超越传统

广东远离中国中原传统文化的直接影响,处处表现出超越传统的文化特点。如惠能以印度佛教为基础创立中国禅宗,康有为提出变君主专制为君主立宪,孙中山提倡民主革命,李小龙带领中国武术走向世界,广东经济特区变计划经济为市场经济,等等,都是超越中原传统文化的例证。

实利重商

自唐宋时期开始,广东就已经成为中国重要的对外贸易区。清朝中期以后,随着国际市场对瓷器、茶叶、丝绸等需求的增加,广东的商品经济得到发展,广东商人尤其是潮汕商人遍布东南亚一带,形成了著名的"潮州帮""广东帮"。商品经济的发展,造就了广东文化实利重商的特点。

2 广东文化的特点
Characteristics of Guangdong Culture

Creativity

Guangdong is far away from Central China; therefore it has been less directly influenced by Central China. This has given Guangdong opportunities surpassing the traditional Chinese culture in many areas, such as Hui Neng who established Southern Chinese Zen Sect based on Buddhism from India, Kang Youwei who called for constitutional monarchy to replace absolute monarchy in the latter age of the Qing Dynasty, Dr. Sun Yat-sen who promoted and led democratic revolution, Bruce Lee who made Chinese martial arts well known worldwide, and last but not least the Special Economic Zones (SEC) in Guangdong which were the earliest innovation transforming the economy from a Planned Economy to a Market Economy in China.

Pro-business

Since the Tang and Song Dynasties, Guangdong has become a very important zone for business and trade with other countries and regions. During the middle reign of the Qing Dynasty, commercial trade in Guangdong was boosted with the increase of the market needs for Chinese porcelains, teas and silks. Guangdong tradesmen and merchants, especially from the Chaoshan area, were widely spread over Southeast Asia, and they formed a number of "Chaozhou Groups" and "Guangdong Groups" everywhere. Guangdong then became very commercially practical while they succeeded in business and trade.

3 广东人

People in Guangdong

广东三大民系 Three Main Ethnic Groups

在中国历史上,中原的汉族迁徙到广东不同地区,与当地人融合,形成广东的广府、潮汕、客家三大民系。广东三大民系各有各的特点。

广府人开放务实

广府人是广东最先形成的一个民系,也最早受到近代西方先进文化和思想的影响,思想上最具有开放性。如今,广府人敢为天下先,使珠江三角洲地区经济迅速发展,成为华南人才的汇聚地。广府人政治观念较弱,而商业意识却很强,具有务实精神,广州商人在清朝中期就已经闻名世界。珠江三角洲是广府人的主要聚居地。

潮汕人精诚团结

韩江三角洲、榕江平原、练江平原、黄冈河三角洲组成潮汕平原,潮汕人就居住在这里。潮汕平原地理环境狭小、资源匮乏。较差的生存环境塑造了潮汕人敢于冒险、勇于开拓、刻苦耐劳等性格特征,其中最为突出的就是强大的凝聚力。潮汕人很早就到我国香港、澳门以及东南亚等地谋生,在异国他乡,潮汕人之间形成了一种彼此照应、互助团结的民风。

3 广东人
People in Guangdong

In Chinese history, the Han Chinese from Central China migrated to different regions in Guangdong and married into other local ethnic groups. As a result, three main ethnic groups were created, known as Cantonese, Chaoshan people, and Hakka, which all have their own characteristics.

Openness and pragmatism of Cantonese

Cantonese are the oldest groups formed in Guangdong, and one of the earliest groups in China influenced by Western culture and ideology so that they are very open-minded. Nowadays, Cantonese are very innovative and dare to try things before others do, which is evident by the rapid economic development of the Pearl River Delta region and a main convergence of talent in Southern China. Cantonese are not keen on politics, but have strong business mind with the pragmatic spirit. Canton businessmen, even in the mid Qing Dynasty, have already been well known around the world. Cantonese mainly settled in the Pearl River Delta area.

Solidarity of Chaoshan people

Chaoshan people live in the Chaoshan Plains, which consist of Hanjiang River Delta, Rongjiang Plain, Lianjiang Plain, and Huanggang River Delta. As a result of poor geographic resources and living environment, people in Chaoshan have been characterized with being adventurous, aggressive, courageous and industrious, especially cohesive. Chaoshan had a long history of travelling to live in places other than their hometown, such as Hong Kong and Macao in China, and Southeast Asian countries. In places other than their hometown, it has become a custom among Chaoshan people that they are willing to help and look after each other.

客家人刻苦自强

俗话说，"逢山必有客，无客不住山。"客家人大都居住在山区，而山区土地非常有限，为了生存，他们不得不经常迁徙。在迁徙过程中，客家人养成一种刻苦耐劳、自立自强的民风。在历史上的多次迁徙中，他们经常整个家族集体迁徙，因而客家人的家族观念特别强烈，这表现在两个方面：一是完善的祠堂设施，连续编撰族谱；二是建造大型的土楼和由众多楼房组合而成的围龙屋。与广府人、潮汕人的重商精神不同，客家人崇尚读书，倡导外出求学，因而有"文化之乡"的美誉。广东三大民系各有各的方言，这些方言都是汉语的方言之一，各种方言之间的差别很大。

Hard working and strong willingness of the Hakka

There is a saying that "where there is a mountain, there is a Hakka; every Hakka will not live away from the mountains." The majority of Hakka live in mountain areas, where there is normally only limited arable land. Therefore, from time to time they had to travel from one area to another in order to survive or have a better life. During migrations, Hakka developed their cultural characteristics of hard working and being strong. For a long time in their migratory history, it was often the case that the whole family would travel to a new land, therefore the Hakka value their family integrity very much. This can be shown by two aspects: the first is the complete ancestral temple facilities and well written and maintained genealogies; the second is big earthen buildings and Round-dragon Houses that consist of a big number of buildings. Different from Cantonese and Chaoshan people who are more keen on business and trade, Hakka people advocate more studying, learning, and encourage travelling abroad for education, and thus the Hakka region has a reputation of the "Hometown of Culture". Each one of these three main ethnic groups has its own dialect, which is a part of the overall Chinese dialects, and there are significant differences among them.

农民工 Migrant Workers

农民工,指身在城市从事非农业工作的农业户口[①]的工人。农民工是中国特有的城乡二元体制的产物。目前,中国农民工的数量达 1.5 亿人左右,主要分布在建筑业、采矿业、第三产业和其他产业链低端或劳动力密集型产业。广东省各个生产领域的产业工人均以农民工为主。农民工为城市发展和经济建设做出了巨大的贡献。

由于各方面的原因,农民工大多数是中国大陆城市最底层的阶层,许多人处于非常艰难的生活和工作状况之中。他们主要从事体力要求较高的建筑工、清洁工、园丁、居民家中的钟点工或保姆、厨师、服务员等脏、累、险、差工种。他们的生活条件差,居住环境差,很多农民工居住在狭窄拥挤的工棚或集体宿舍里,周边环境肮脏零乱。所

---

①户口是中国独有的一种人口管理方法。一个中国人出生后被要求选择其父母中的一方的户籍作为自己的户籍。一般有农业户口和非农业户口之分。

3 广东人
People in Guangdong

Migrant workers are those who have an agricultural household registration① but live in cities and are engaged in non-agricultural work. They are the new group of a Chinese special urban-rural dual system. At present, the number of migrant workers in China has reached about 150 million and they are mainly working in building industry, mining, tertiary industries or other labour-intensive industries. Now migrant workers have become the major working force in all manufacturing and production areas in Guangdong Province, and they have made tremendous contributions to Guangdong urban and economic development.

Because of different reasons, most of migrant workers are the lowest paid working classes in the Chinese mainland cities and in very hard living and working condition. They mainly work in high physically demanding types of job, such as construction workers, cleaners, gardeners, full-time or part-time nannies, cooks, waiters and waitress or other jobs that maybe dirty, dangerous, or poorly paid. In general, they face poor living conditions and environments and many migrant workers live in crowded barracks or dormitories with dirty and messy surroundings. Their employers normally pay them low salaries,

---

① Household registration is unique to China as a population management approach. There are two different accounting conditions at present: one being a rural and the other being an urban residence. After a child is born, the parents are asked to choose one of the parents' residences as the child's main residence.

在单位提供工资待遇比较低,大部分农民工不能享受住房补贴[1]或住房公积金[2],不能带薪休假,女性农民工无法享受带薪休产假的待遇。城市医疗保险体系没有覆盖到农民工,发生疾病或工伤时,不能享受医疗保险。缺少最基本的文化娱乐方式,精神上缺乏与外界的沟通和交流。农民工的子女没有城市户口,他们无法在城市接受教育。

可喜的是,中国政府正在逐步采取措施,统一城乡户籍制度,从根本上解决农民工面临的问题。

---

[1]住房补贴是中国政府为解决职工的住房问题而给予的补贴,也就是把单位本来用于建房、购房的资金转化为住房补贴,分次(如按月)或者一次性地发给职工,再由职工到市场上购买或者租赁住房。

[2]住房公积金是单位及其在职职工缴存的长期住房储金,是住房分配货币化、社会化和法制化的主要形式。

3 广东人
People in Guangdong

and most of them cannot enjoy housing allowances [1] and funds [2]. Most of migrant workers cannot take paid annual leave and female migrant workers cannot enjoy paid maternity leave like others. They are not covered by urban medical insurance systems, so they cannot claim costs when they become ill or injured during working hours. They also lack the most basic entertainment and communication channels with the outside world. Furthermore, children of migrant workers without urban household registration cannot receive free education in the city.

It is good to see that the Chinese government is making efforts and actions to gradually unify the urban and rural household registration systems, aiming at fundamentally resolving the problems migrant workers face today.

---

[1] Housing allowances are allowances provided by government for workers who has difficulties in buying a house. Instead using the housing fund for household development or purchase of public estate, but giving individuals allowances in installment (for example monthly) or once for all, helping the individuals buying house from the market.

[2] The housing fund is a long-term housing savings deposited by both the employer and the employee, which is the main form of monetization, socialization and legalization of housing allocation.

广东老外 Foreigners in Guangdong

广东是一个国际化的省份,广东省的很多城市都是国际化的大都市。在广州市常住的外国人约有2万人,临时居住的外国人每年约50万人;深圳市常住的外国人约有1.3万人;在东莞市常住的外国人约有1万人;在珠海市常住的外国人约有3000多人。另外,每年在广东的留学生有1.4万多人。

他们在广东的生活面临着一些问题,如广州市目前只有一家针对外国人的加美医院,而且只提供英、日、德三种语言服务。广州市越秀区是外国人最集中的城区,但因很多外国人不懂中国话,无法与本地人沟通而产生矛盾。

针对这种情况,广州市越秀区政府对辖区保安进行简单的英语会话培训,以方便交流沟通;东莞市政府编写了《外国人在莞指南》一书,提供与外籍人士有关的出入境、居住、商业法规、旅游休闲等信息,为在东莞的外国人带来帮助和便利;广东省政府还规定,来广东工作、学习满一年的外国人可以在广东购买住房。

3 广东人
People in Guangdong

Guangdong is an international province; there are a number of metropolises within Guangdong alone, and there are about 20,000 permanent foreign residents in Guangzhou and about half a million temporary foreign residents each year; there are about 13 thousand foreigner residents in Shenzhen; about 10 thousand in Dongguan and about 3,000 in Zhuhai. Apart from the above mentioned, there are more than 14 thousand foreign students in Guangdong each year.

They also face some daily problems living in Guangdong. For example, there is only one hospital (Guangzhou Can Am International Medical Center) for foreigners in Guangzhou, which only provides English, Japanese and German language services. Yuexiu District has the largest foreigner population in Guangzhou. However many of them do not speak Chinese, thus are incapable of communicating with the local people.

In view of this, the Yuexiu District Government has been providing basic training of English conversation skill to security guards. Dongguan Municipal Government has published *The Guide to Foreigners in Dongguan*, a booklet providing information about immigration, living, business regulations, tourism, and leisure in order to help foreigners. Guangdong Provincial Government issued a regulation allowing foreigners, who have lived or studied in Guangdong for more than a year, to purchase a residential housing.

4 广东人的生活

People's Daily Life in Guangdong

凉茶 Herbal Tea

"凉茶"不是茶,而是中草药熬出来的药汤,是中草药植物性饮料的通称。广东凉茶是中国凉茶的代表。

由于广东地区气候潮湿炎热,所以生活在广东的人容易"上火①"。广东人把一些清热解毒、消暑去湿的草药配制成各式各样的凉茶,常常饮用,尤其是在夏天,当作清凉饮料饮用。除了清热解毒外,凉茶还有祛湿、生津、清火、明目、散结、消肿等作用,可以治疗目赤头痛、头晕耳鸣、疔疮肿毒和高血压等疾病。凉茶可以煮也可以泡。虽然凉茶只需要煮5~10分钟时间,但等它凉了再喝却要花很长时间。为了节省时间,可以往煮好的凉茶里加一些凉的开水,这并不影响凉茶的功效。

体质偏寒凉的人不宜多喝凉茶,孕妇、儿童、老年人也不适合喝凉茶。除此之外,隔夜的凉茶不能喝。另外,凉茶毕竟是药,不能乱喝,更不能作为保健药长期饮用。

常见的凉茶品牌有王老吉、和其正、邓老凉茶、霸王、黄振龙、致中和等。

---

① "上火"是中医术语,意为人体阴阳失衡,内火旺盛。所谓的"火"是形容身体内某些热性的症状。而上火也就是人体阴阳失衡后出现的内热症,在体内形成"湿毒"。

"Herbal tea" (Cool tea in Chinese language) is not actually a kind of tea, but is a general name for herbal beverages, which is stewed from boiled herbs. Guangdong herbal tea is a typical representative of Chinese herbal teas.

Due to the hot and humid climate in Guangdong, Guangdong people believe that "agony or internal heat [1] tends to be built up and "dampness toxins" formed in the body. They make a variety of herbal teas made of some herbs having medical functions of detoxification and refreshing dehumidification; then drink the teas from time to time as cool beverages, especially in summer time. In addition to detoxification and refreshing dehumidification, the herbal teas also have the properties of promoting the production of fluids, removing heat-phlegm, improving eyesight, dissolving hard masses, detumescence, etc. It helps to cure illnesses such as sore-eye and headache, dizziness and tinnitus, boils and swelling, and hypertension. Herbal teas can be prepared by boiling or steeping. It takes normally 5–10 minutes to make a pot of tea, but it may take much longer time waiting for it to cool down, so you can always add some cool boiled water into the hot tea, which will not reduce its effects.

A person who has a cold constitution should not drink too many herbal teas, and they are not suitable for pregnant women, children and aged people. It is also believed that it is not good for the health to drink overnight herbal teas. Note that herbal teas are actually made of medical herbs, and need to be consumed with care and should not be used as health care products and consumed over long periods of time.

Some well-known herbal tea brands include Wanglaoji, Heqizheng, Denglao Liangcha, Bawang, Huangzhenlong, and Zhizhonghe, etc.

---

[1] The "internal heat" is a Chinese Medicine term. It means Yin-Yang imbalance inside one's body, specifically with dominance of "internal fire". The so-called "fire" describes the symptom of some kind of inner heat so the "internal heat" is the "inner heat illness" due to Yin-Yang imbalance inside the body."

靓汤 Soup

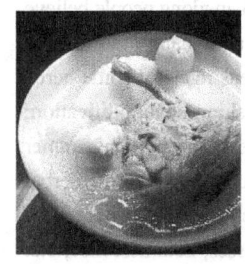

一般人认为，中国人见面的时候喜欢问"吃了吗？"但广东人见面时却可能会说"喝汤了吗？"俗话说："宁可食无菜，不可食无汤。"老火靓汤是广东人生活中最常见的饮食文化。"先上汤、后上菜"几乎成为广东宴席的固定程序。

老火靓汤一般用瓦罐来煲，水开以后，先放进汤料，再煮开，然后把火调小，最后慢慢熬2~4小时。广东人喜欢用新鲜的材料替代干药引子①，比如猪肺、霸王花、瘦肉、猪骨等。酒店就更讲究，经常用乌龟、甲鱼、乳鸽、乌鸡、蛇、鱼翅、鲍鱼、干贝等做药引子。常见的辅料则有党参、沙参、枸杞、红枣、人参、花旗参、姜片等。

其实，老火靓汤来源于中医的一种食补方法。广东一带地气湿热，长时间居住在这里，热毒、湿气容易侵身，为了祛湿解毒，如果喝真正的汤药，味道很苦。根据中药的煎熬方法，广东人研制出既有中药功效又好喝的老火靓汤。可见，在广东人看来，汤和中药基本上是一样的。虽然广东的老火靓汤很好喝，但也不能喝太多，和中药一样，喝多了没有好处，反而有害。

著名的广东靓汤有罗汉果白菜干汤、木瓜花生排骨汤、鲤鱼乌豆汤、老鸭汤，等等。

---

①药引子指某些药物能引导其他药物的效力到达病变部位或者某一经脉，起"引导"的作用。

4 广东人的生活
People's Daily Life in Guangdong

It is a custom that when Chinese people meet, they like to ask "eaten yet?" (as a greeting similar to "hello"). However, Cantonese will ask "soup yet?" There is a saying in Guangdong that "Prefer to a meal without a dish, rather than a meal without soup."

The "old fire" (slow-cooked) soup is the most common food culture in Guangdong. "The soup first then the main course" is almost the fixed Guangdong meal order. The "old fire" soup is normally cooked in a crock (earthen jar). First put the soup herbs in boiling water, bring it back to boil and then simmer using a small fire for two to four hours. Guangdong people also love to use fresh materials as "Yao Yinzi ①" instead of dry herbs, such as pig lung, king spent (a kind of cactus), lean pork, pork bones. Restaurants use even more expensive materials like turtles, squabs, black chickens, snakes, shark's fin, abalones, scallops, etc. Codonopsis, radix, wolfberry, red dates, ginseng, American ginseng, ginger, etc. are often used as enhancement ingredients.

In fact, the "old fire" soup is originated from a kind of Chinese medicine practice, improving health with foods. It is humid and hot in Guangdong area and heat and dampness are harmful to health, so one needs to drink herbal soup for detoxification and refreshing dehumidification, but normally herbal soups are very bitter. Guangdong people invented this method of making soup in the same way as making herbal soups, which is tasty and has the same medical effects with the herbal soups. In the eyes of Guangdong people, soups and Chinese herbal medicines are almost the same. It is advised that the "old fire" soups are tasty and delicious, but need to be consumed sensibly. It is harmful if too much is taken at one time.

The well-known Guangdong soups include Mangosteen Soup with Dry Cabbage, Pork Ribs Soup with Papaya and Peanut, Carp Soup with Black Bean, Old Duck Soup, just to name a few.

---

① Yao Yinzi: Certain drugs can lead other drugs to reach the lesion or a meridian.

糖水 Sweet Soup

糖水是广东一种小吃的总称，种类多样。既可以作为饭后的甜品，也可以作为夜宵的小吃，非常受广东人欢迎。

糖水跟靓汤一样，具有滋补养生的功效。广东人认为，广东一带湿热，容易使人"上火"，因此就把一些"下火"的东西和糖放在水里一起煮，喝了之后消暑。研究表明，在烦躁、不容易入眠的时候，喝糖水可使体内产生大量血清素，帮助睡眠。同时，有些糖水也有一定的止咳作用。

常见的糖水有番薯糖水、木瓜银耳糖水、海带绿豆糖水、莲子百合银耳汤、水果西米露、姜撞奶、冰糖燕窝、双皮奶，等等。下面介绍一种清热解暑糖水的做法。

莲子百合银耳汤

原料：莲子100克、干银耳15克、新鲜百合120克、香蕉2根、枸杞5克、冰糖100克

做法：

1. 把干银耳泡在水里2个小时，去除老蒂和杂质，撕成小瓣，加4杯水放进蒸笼蒸半个小时后取出备用；

2. 新鲜百合拔开洗干净，去除老蒂；

3. 把香蕉洗干净，去皮，切成3毫米厚的薄片；

4. 将所有材料放入炖盅中，加调味料，放进蒸笼蒸30分钟即可。

Sweet soup is a general name for a variety of Cantonese light side dishes. It is one of the favorites of Cantonese and is served either as a dessert after a meal or as evening tea.

Similar to the "old fire" soup, the sweet soup is beneficial to health. Cantonese believe that it is easy for a person in Guangdong feel "agony"

because of humid and hot weather. Drinking the sweet soup made by using something cool with sugar can help remove the "agony". Some research reports also indicate that it helps sleep if one is irritated and can not fall asleep easily, because drinking sweet soup can help produce serotonin in the body facilitating sleep. Sweet soup also helps in stopping coughs.

The most common sweet soups include Sweet Potato Soup; Soup with Papaya and Tremella; Soup with Kelp and Green Beans; Soup with Lotus, Lily and Tremella; Fruited Sago; Fresh Milk with Ginger; Bird's Nest with Crystal Sugar; Double-layered Steamed Milk, etc. The following is a recipe of soup for detoxification and refreshing dehumidification.

Soup with Lotus, Lily and Tremella

Ingredients: lotus seeds, 100 grams; dried tremella, 15 grams; fresh lilies, 120 grams; two bananas; wolfberry, 5 grams; and crystal sugar, 100 grams

Steps:

1. Dip tremella in the water for two hours, remove tough pedicles and impurities, tear it into small pieces and then put them into a bowl with 4 cups of water. Then steam it for half an hour.

2. Wash the fresh lilies and remove the tough pedicles.

3. Peel the bananas then cut them into about 3 millimetres thick slices.

4. Put all the above into a steam pot then steam them another half an hour. It is then ready to serve.

早茶 Morning Tea

每到周末或者节假日，你都可以在广州的茶楼看到扶老携幼、三五成群的广州人在"叹早茶"。粤语"叹"是享受的意思。

广州早茶的茶水以红茶为主，红茶有暖胃去腻、帮助消化的作用。常见的红茶有乌龙茶、铁观音、普洱茶。有的人也喜欢在普洱茶中加入菊花（菊普茶），有清凉祛火的功效。喝早茶适合朋友聚会、洽谈生意、业余消遣。

喝早茶要吃茶点。茶点分为干湿两种，干点有饺子、粉果、包子、酥点等，湿点有粥类、肉类、龟苓膏、豆腐花等。其中干点做得最精致，卖得最好。

广州人一般喜欢在茶楼喝早茶。茶楼也是广州最有代表性的、最传统的吃早餐的地方。喝茶时，必须先给别人倒茶，最后才倒给自己。别人给你倒茶时，要用食指和中指轻叩桌面表示感谢。据说这一习俗来源于清朝皇帝乾隆下江南的故事。传说他到江南视察时，曾微服私访，有一次来到一家茶楼，一时高兴，竟给跟随他的仆人倒茶。按皇宫的

4 广东人的生活
People's Daily Life in Guangdong

Every weekend or in public holidays, one can always see in the restaurants that many Cantonese, old or young, in groups "Tan" morning tea. "Tan" simply means "enjoy" in Cantonese.

Tea itself in morning tea in Guangzhou is mainly a kind of "black tea", which is good for the stomach and helps digestion. The most common black teas include Oolong, Tie Guanyin, and Pu'er. Some people also like to add chrysanthemum into Pu'er, which can help to remove internal heat. It is a good time during morning tea time to meet with friends or business partners and also entertain guests.

People normally eat dim sum during morning tea. There are dry and wet categories of dim sum. Dumplings, buns and bakeries (tarts and pies) belong to the dry category, while porridges, meat dishes, Guiling Jelly and Bean Curd desserts are typical wet ones. Normally the dry dim sum is more delicate and appealing, hence more popular.

Cantonese normally like to go to "Tea Restaurants" for the morning tea. Tea Restaurants are traditionally the most common places for breakfast. During tea time, one needs to serve the tea for others first before serving himself. While being served, one needs to tap on the table using the forefinger and middle finger together, meaning "thank you". It is from a folk story of Emperor Qianlong, who visited Jiangnan (Jiangsu and Zhejiang Provinces)

规矩，仆人必须跪着接受。但为了不暴露乾隆的身份，仆人将食指和中指弯曲，做成屈膝的姿势，轻叩桌面，代替下跪。后来逐渐演变成广州人喝茶时的一种礼仪。

海外华人中的广东人特别多，他们把广州早茶带到了世界各地。在东南亚、欧美等地都可以找到广东茶楼，喝到广州早茶。

4 广东人的生活
People's Daily Life in Guangdong

during the Qing Dynasty. According to the story, Qianlong secretly cruised to Jiangnan wearing common costumes. One day, he and his servants came to a tea restaurant. Being very excited, he served a cup of tea to one of his servants. According to the rules in the Forbidden City, the servant must kneel down to receive the honor in this case. However, the royal status of the emperor must be kept secret, so the servant tapped on the table with his forefinger and middle finger mimicking the kneeling posture. It was then adopted as a custom of courtesy among the Cantonese.

There is a big population of Guangdong people among overseas Chinese people, and they bring Cantonese morning tea to places all over the world. Now you can find many Cantonese Tea Restaurants in Southeast Asia, Europe, and America and they all enjoy Cantonese morning tea (dim sum) daily.

粤菜 Cantonese Cuisine

俗话说，"吃在广州。"粤菜，是中国著名的八大菜系之一，包括广州菜、潮州菜、东江菜，其中广州菜最有名。粤菜或许是用料最广泛、做法最丰富的一个菜系。"天上的除了飞机，地上的除了桌子，水中的除了轮船"，几乎都可以拿来做菜，如鹧鸪、禾花雀、豹狸、果子狸、穿山甲、海狗、老鼠、乌龟，等等。广东人还特别喜欢吃海鲜、河鲜、鱼蛤虫蛇。

粤菜注重质和味，口味比较清淡，并且随着季节的变化而变化，夏、秋偏重清淡，冬、春偏重浓郁，追求色、香、味、型。调味包含酸、甜、苦、辣、咸，味道讲究清、鲜、嫩、爽、滑、香，被称为"五滋六味"。著名的粤菜有白切贵妃鸡、龙虎斗、护国菜、文昌鸡、盐焗鸡、满汉全席、醉虾、醉蟹、西汁乳鸽等。

据介绍，目前美国有上万家中国餐馆，英国有4000家，日本有数千家，法国、荷兰各有2000多家。这些地方的中餐馆，大多数是粤式茶楼、菜馆，生意很好。"吃在广州"蜚声海内外。

白切贵妃鸡

清蒸东星斑

西汁乳鸽

4 广东人的生活
People's Daily Life in Guangdong

There is a saying "Eating in Guangzhou is the best." Cantonese cuisine is one of Eight Major Cuisines in China. It includes Guangzhou dishes, Chaozhou dishes, and Dongjiang dishes, among them the Guangzhou dishes are the most famous. Cantonese cuisine is perhaps the one using the most different types of techniques and most varieties of materials. It is said that "The exceptions are aeroplanes in the sky, tables on ground, and ships in the sea." Actually almost every single edible thing can be used for cooking, such as partridges, sparrows, fox leopards, civet cats, pangolins, fur seals, mice, turtles. Cantonese also in particular like seafood, freshwater fishes, shell fishes, and even snakes.

The quality and taste are the key factors in Cantonese cuisine. The taste is normally relatively light but changes with the season. During summer and autumn the emphasis is lighter, but in winter and spring time it tends to be more flavoured. The integration of colours, flavours, tastes and decorations is also state of the art. The taste normally needs to be clear, fresh, tender, cool, smooth, and fragrant, and flavours can be sour, sweet, bitter, spicy, and salty, known as the "Five-flavours and Six-tastes". Some famous Cantonese cuisines are Sliced Boiled Chicken, Dragon Fights Tiger (cooked cat and snake), Huguo Dishes, Wenchang Chicken, Salt-Baked Chicken, Man-Han Feast, Drunk Prawns, Drunk Crabs and Pigeon with Western Sauce, etc.

According to reports, there are more than ten thousand Chinese restaurants in the United States alone, 4,000 in United Kingdom, several thousands in Japan, and a couple of thousand in France and Netherlands respectively. Most of Chinese restaurants in the above mentioned countries and areas are Cantonese restaurants, and their business is very good. "One should eat in Guangzhou" becomes well-known at home and abroad.

粤语 Yue Dialect

粤语又叫白话、广府话。粤语是一种属汉藏语系汉语族的声调语言。它的名称来源于中国古代对岭南的称谓"越"（通"粤"），是中国大陆仅次于官方语言（普通话①）的一种语言；主要分布在中国广东省中西部地区及珠江三角洲地区、广西中南部及东南部地区、香港、澳门等，东南亚的印尼北苏门答腊省棉兰市、圣诞岛、马来西亚、越南，以及北美、英国、澳大利亚和新西兰等华人（粤人）社区。

粤语由中国的古代汉语演变而来，它的形成与发展经历了一个长期的过程。另一方面，它也吸收了一些南方非汉语的成分，与普通话和其他方言有比较大的差异，具有独特的语音特点，但语法和词汇基本相同。

目前全球使用粤语的人口大约有 1.3 亿，使用地区比较广泛，其中广东约 7000 万，广西 3000 多万，港澳台同胞和海外华人华侨约 1000 万人。

以粤语为基础形成的粤剧、粤曲、粤语流行歌曲、粤语电视剧、粤语电影影响着除广东、香港之外的中国内地的非粤语省市。目前，广东电视台、广播电台的某些频道或节目以粤语为播音语言，这在全国都是绝无仅有的。为了工作需要，许多人正在争相学习粤语。

---

①普通话指以北京语音为标准音，以北方话为基础方言，以典范的现代白话文作品为语法规范，是通行于中国大陆、香港、澳门、台湾各地人们以及海外华人的共同语言，并作为教学、媒体等的官方语言。普通话是中国的官方语言，也是联合国六种官方工作语言之一。

4 广东人的生活
People's Daily Life in Guangdong

Cantonese (Yue Dialect) is also known as Baihua Dialect or Guangfu Dialect. It is one of the Sino-Tibetan languages. Its name is derived from the ancient name Yue of the Lingnan area. It is only second to the official language, Mandarin or Putonghua[①], in the mainland China. The main Cantonese speakers are from the Mid-west of Guangdong Province, Pearl River Delta, Mid-south and Southeast of Guangxi Province, Hong Kong, Macao, and other regions in China. The Cantonese speakers also include overseas Chinese from Medan City, North Sumatra Province, Indonesia, Christmas Island, Malaysia, Vietnam in Southeast Asia and North America, Britain, Australia and New Zealand, etc.

Cantonese has evolved from ancient Chinese language, its formation and development have gone through a long process. On the other hand, it also absorbed some of the southern non-Chinese elements, and then became very different from Mandarin and other dialects, with its own unique phonetic characteristics, however with much the same grammar and vocabulary.

Currently the number of Cantonese speakers is about 130 million all over the world, including about 70 million in Guangdong, more than 30 million in Guangxi, and about 10 million in Hong Kong, Macao, Taiwan and other parts of the world.

Cantonese opera, music, pop music, television series, and movies have the widest coverage over Guangdong, Hong Kong and many non-Cantonese provinces and cities in mainland China. At present, some Guangdong TV and radio channels and programs broadcast in Cantonese only, which is unique in China. More and more people are now keen to learn Cantonese for work.

---

① Putonghua (Mandarin) refers to the common language spoken by people from mainland China, Hong Kong, Macao, Taiwan and overseas Chinese, and as an official language for teaching and the media, which is based on northern dialects and pronunciation of Beijing, and its grammar specification on the modern vernacular works. Mandarin is the official language of China, and also one of the six United Nations official working languages.

5 广东主要城市

Major Cities in Guangdong

广州 Guangzhou

广州简称穗，又叫羊城、穗城、花城，是广东省的省会，已经有2200多年的历史，是海上丝绸之路的起点，被称为中国的"南大门"。中国的第三大河（珠江）从广州市区穿流而过，因此广州市内岛屿很多。广州是继北京、上海之后的中国第三大城市，也是中国华侨数量最多的城市。全市面积7434.4平方公里，常住人口超过1200万。广州又是中国最主要的对外开放城市之一，生活在广州的外国人很多。

位于越秀公园内的五羊石像是广州市的标志，也是市内最著名的景点之一。传说在周朝时，南海飘来五朵彩云，五位仙人骑着五只羊，分别携带一串谷穗降临广州，赠送谷穗给居民，祝福这里五谷丰登，留下的五只羊化为石头。广州因此而得名"羊城""穗城"。2010年第16届广州亚洲运动会会徽就是以五羊石像为基础而设计的。因为广州气候温暖，四季鲜花盛开，所以又叫"花城"。

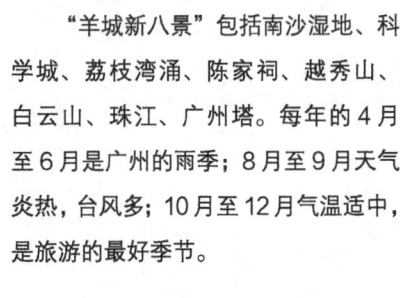

"羊城新八景"包括南沙湿地、科学城、荔枝湾涌、陈家祠、越秀山、白云山、珠江、广州塔。每年的4月至6月是广州的雨季；8月至9月天气炎热，台风多；10月至12月气温适中，是旅游的最好季节。

5 广东主要城市
Major Cities in Guangdong

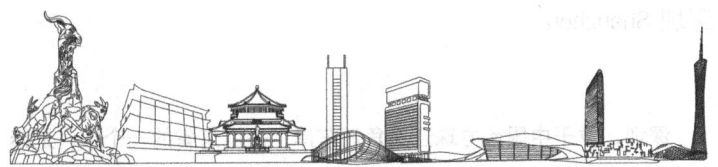

Guangzhou is the capital city of Guangdong Province, and it is also known as "Goat City", "Sui (Sui means grains) City" and "Flower City". It has more than 2,200-year history. It is the starting point of the Maritime Silk Road and therefore refereed to as the South Gate of China. The third biggest river in China, Pearl River, flows through the city centre, so there are many small isles inside Guangzhou City. It is also the third largest city in China today, after Beijing and Shanghai. The city area is 7,434.4 square kilometres, and the resident population is more than 12 million. Guangzhou is one of China's leading open cities, and there are a great number of foreigners living in the city.

Located in Yuexiu Park, Guangzhou Wuyang (Five Goats) Stone Statue is the symbol of Guangzhou and is also one of the most famous landmarks. There is an old myth in which five gods came to that place by riding five goats. They gave some grains to the commoners and blessed those people who lived there and the hunger and starvation ended. The gods returned to heaven and left the five goats which turned into stone. The city is hence named "Goat City" and "Sui City". The emblem of "16th Asian Games Guangzhou 2010" is designed based on the Wuyang Stone Statue. The city is also known as "Flower City" because it has flowers blooming in all seasons due to the warm sub-tropical climate.

"Eight New Sights of Guangzhou" include Nansha Moors, Science City, Lizhiwan Channel, Chen Clan Temple, Yuexiu Mountain, Baiyun Mountain, the Pearl River and Canton Tower. The rainy season is from April to June, and it is hot and has typhoons in August and September. The best time for tourists to travel in Guangzhou is between October and December when the weather is mild and pleasant.

深圳 Shenzhen

深圳，位于中国南方珠江三角洲东岸，是广东省的一个市，是继北京、上海、广州之后的中国第四大城市。全市总面积2020平方公里，全市常住人口超过1000万。当地的方言（客家话）把田野间的水沟称为"圳"或"涌"。深圳正因为有很多河流，而且村子旁边有一条很深的水沟，所以叫作"深圳"。

1980年8月26日，中国政府批准在深圳设立中国第一个经济特区①，因此，这一天也被称为"深圳的生日"。从2010年7月1日起特区范围扩大到全市。经过30多年的建设和发展，如今的深圳已经由一个昔日的边陲小渔村发展成为具有巨大国际影响力的现代化大都市，创造了举世瞩目的"深圳速度"②。深圳是中国口岸最多和唯一拥有海陆空口岸的城市，是中国高新技术产业基地、信息中心、商贸中心、运输中心，全球第五大金融中心。2008年，深圳被授予"设计之都"称号，成为全球第六个"设计之都"。

---

①经济特区是中国政府允许外国公民、华侨、港澳台同胞及其公司、企业进行投资活动并实行特殊政策的地区。

②"深圳速度"是中国形容建设速度非常快的一个词语。这个词语出现在1982年11月—1985年12月的37个月期间，中国一家公司在承建深圳国际贸易中心大厦时，创下了三天盖一层楼的速度。该大厦的建设过程成为深圳城市建设的一个典型而广为人知。因此，深圳快速的城市建设和发展被称为"深圳速度"。

5 广东主要城市
Major Cities in Guangdong

Shenzhen, one of the cities in Guangdong, is located on the east bank of the Pearl River, and it is the fourth largest city in China after Beijing, Shanghai and Guangzhou. The city has a total area of 2,020 square kilometres with a resident population of over 10 million. A ditch between fields is called a "zhen" in Hakka, the main local dialect. Because there are many rivers in the area, and there is also a very deep ditch by the village, the village was named Shenzhen (meaning deep ditch).

On August 26, 1980, the very first Special Economic Zone (SEZ) [1] in China was approved by the Chinese government and established in Shenzhen, and the day is also called the birthday of the city. From July 1, 2010 the whole city became a SEC. After 30 years of construction and developments, today, Shenzhen is a modern international metropolis which has evolved from an old-time fishing village and has been created with remarkable "Shenzhen Speed" [2]. Shenzhen is the only Chinese city with sea, land and air ports, which is also a high-tech industry base, information centre, business centre, transportation centre and the world's fifth largest financial centre. Shenzhen was awarded the title of "City of Design" in 2008, and now it is the sixth biggest "Design City" in the world.

---

① Special Economic Zone is the area in which Chinese government applies a special policy for absorbing investment activities from foreign nationals and overseas chinese, compatriots from Hong Kong, Macao and Taiwan, as well as their companies and enterprises.

② "Shenzhen Speed" is a phrase in China representing rapid development. The phrase appeared during the 37 months between November 1982 and December 1985. Shenzhen International Trade Centre was built by one construction company with a pace equaled to building one storey every 3 days. This building became widely known as the symbol of Shenzhen city development; hence the fast pace of Shenzhen city development is phrased as "Shenzhen Speed".

广东文化与社会
Cantonese Culture and Society

深圳是客家人的主要聚居地之一，约有400万客家人生活在深圳，客家话、粤语是深圳本地的方言。改革开放之后，中国各地的大量移民进入深圳，普通话成为最通用的语言。

深圳一年四季都适合旅游，尤其以冬天和早春为最佳。

5 广东主要城市
Major Cities in Guangdong

Shenzhen is one of the main settlements of Hakka people, and about 4 million Hakka people live in the area. The local main dialects are Hakka and Cantonese (Baihua Dialect). After the reform and opening-up, a large number of immigrants came to Shenzhen from all over of China, and Mandarin then became the most common language.

It is good all year round to visit Shenzhen. However, winter and early spring are the best seasons.

广东文化与社会
Cantonese Culture and Society

珠海 Zhuhai

珠海,在中国南方珠江三角洲南端,因位于珠江入南海处而得名。陆地面积1701平方公里,海洋面积6135平方公里,全市常住人口150多万,是广东省人口最少的城市。珠海海岸线长604公里,有146个岛屿,有"百岛之市"的美称。珠海曾被联合国授予"联合国改善人居环境最佳范例奖"。

1980年,中国政府批准珠海成立经济特区,特区面积6.81平方公里。2010年,珠海经济特区范围扩大到全市。珠海的主要工业包括电子及通信设备、电子仪器及机械、办公设备。珠海每两年举行一次的中国国际航空航天博览会是国际性专业航空航天展览,是世界五大航展之一,展览包括实物展示、飞行表演、贸易洽谈、学术交流,简称"珠海航展"。珠海航展面向公众开放。

5 广东主要城市
Major Cities in Guangdong

Zhuhai is located in the south of the Pearl River Delta and is named for its geographical location at the mouth of Pearl River which flows into the South China Sea (Sea is pronounced as "Hai" in Chinese). It has a land territory of 1,701 square kilometres and sea area of 6,135 square kilometres. The resident population is now about 1.5 million and is the least populated city in Guangdong Province. Zhuhai has coastline of 604 kilometres with 146 islands; hence also nicknamed "City of Hundred Islands". The city was once awarded "International Award for Best Practices to Improve the Living Environment" given out by the UN.

In 1980, Zhuhai established its first Special Economy Zone (SEZ) with an area of only 6.81 square kilometres, however, the SEZ has already covered the whole city area since 2010. The main manufacturing industries in Zhuhai include electronics and communication instruments, electronic equipment and machinery, as well as office equipment. Biennial China (Zhuhai) International Aviation and Aerospace Exhibition (namely Airshow China) is an international professional exhibition for the aviation and aerospace industry, which is one of the five biggest exhibitions of its kind. The exhibition provides product displays, air shows, trade meetings, and academic seminars, and it is open to the public.

在珠海，你可以"住海边、玩海面、吃海鲜"。珠海的海鲜非常多，有几条很有名的海鲜一条街，如拱北迎宾北路一带、香洲沿河路至唐家湾一带、九洲港路段、新香洲怡华街等；水湾路的酒吧一条街也远近闻名。

珠海的城市标志是珠海渔女，位于香炉湾畔。传说南海龙王的第七个女儿小玉龙在南海附近游玩时，被珠海香炉湾美丽的风光所吸引，不愿返回龙宫，决定来到人间，就化身渔女和当地的一个渔民结婚，从此留在珠海。

In Zhuhai, one can be "living by the sea, having fun by the sea, and eating seafood from the sea". There is a variety of seafood in Zhuhai, and a number of "sea food streets" which are very popular, including Yingbin Road North, the street from Xiangzhou River Bank to Tangjiawan, Jiuzhougang Road, and Yihua Street in Xinxiangzhou District. Shuiwan Bar Street is also well-known.

The symbol of Zhuhai is the Zhuhai Fisher Girl, which is located by Xianglu Bay. According to the legend, she was the Jade Dragon, the seventh daughter of the Dragon King of the South China Sea. One day she was having fun near the South China Sea and was attracted by the beautiful scenery of Xianglu Bay, thus unwilling to return to the Dragon Palace under the sea. So she decided to stay on the land, then turned herself into a fisher girl and married a local fisherman, living happily in Zhuhai thereafter.

中山 Zhongshan

中山,古代叫香山,位于中国南方珠江三角洲的中南部,是广东省的一个市。全市总面积1783.67平方公里,常住人口310多万。中山市曾获得"联合国人居奖"。

1866年11月12日,中国伟大的民主革命先行者孙中山诞生在中山市南朗镇翠亨村。为了纪念孙中山,香山县于1925年改名为中山县;1983年,中山市设立,这是中国唯一一座以伟人名字命名的城市。中山市也是中国著名的侨乡,有旅居世界87个国家和地区的海外侨胞、港澳台同胞80多万人。

中山主要使用汉语方言,包括粤语、闽南话、客家话。其中使用粤语的人数最多。

中山市最适合旅游的季节是春季和秋季。

5 广东主要城市
Major Cities in Guangdong

Zhongshan, located in the central and southern Pearl River Delta region, is another city of Guangdong Province. It was called Xiangshan in the past, with a territory of 1,783.67 square kilometres and more than 3.1 million residents nowadays. Zhongshan City has previously received the UN Habitat Award.

The great Chinese democratic revolution forerunner Dr. Sun Yat-sen was born in Tsui Hang Village, Nam Long Town, Zhongshan City (was known as Xiangshan County at the time), on November 12, 1866. Xiangshan County was renamed Zhongshan County in 1925 for commemorating Dr. Sun Yat-sen. Then Zhongshan County received its city status and became Zhongshan City in 1983. It is the only city named after a great figure in China. Zhongshan City is one of the most famous hometowns of overseas Chinese. Today there are more than 800 thousand overseas Chinese and compatriots in Hong Kong, Macao, Taiwan, spreading over 87 countries and regions.

The main dialects in Zhongshan are Cantonese, Minnan (Southern Min) and Hakka, and most people speak Cantonese.

The best time for visiting the city is spring and autumn.

东莞 Dongguan

东莞,位于中国南方珠江口东岸、东江下游的珠江三角洲。全市陆地面积2465平方公里,海岸线长115.94公里,海域面积150平方公里,浅海滩涂面积45平方公里。全市常住人口超过1000万。截止到2011年,港澳同胞约100万人,海外华侨约30万人,是中国著名的侨乡。因盛产莞草而被称为"东莞"。

号称"世界工厂"的东莞,拥有全球最大的制造业基地、羊毛衫生产基地、UPS制造基地,拥有中国家具出口第一镇、第一个服装设计制造基地和最大的汽配城。东莞经济尤其是以外向型工业为主,在全球经济500强城市中排名前200,拥有全球500强企业45家,境外上市公司800多家。著名企业包括美国的杜邦,瑞士的雀巢,荷兰的菲利浦,德国的赫司特,法国的汤姆逊,韩国的三星,日本的日立、新日铁、索尼、住友金属,英国的太古集团,芬兰的诺基亚,等等。

Dongguan City is located on the east coast of the Pearl River estuary and downstream of the East River in the Pearl River Delta region in southern China. The city has a land area of about 2,465 square kilometres with 115.94 kilometres coastline, 150 square kilometres sea area and 45 square kilometres beach area. The resident population of the city is more than 10 million. As of 2011, there are about one million people from Dongguan living in Hong Kong and Macao and about 300 thousand overseas; therefore it is well-known as the hometown of overseas Chinese. The city's name "Dongguan" actually comes from its richness of Guan Grass (Water Sedge).

Known as the "World's Factory", Dongguan has the world largest manufacturing base, production base of sweaters, and UPS manufacturing base and also possesses the leading town of Chinese furniture for exports and fashion design, and the largest automobile parts manufacturer. Dongguan's economy is export-oriented and currently enjoys the top 200 position of the global top 500 economy cities. It contains 45 companies within the list of Fortune 500 and more than 800 overseas listed companies. The high profile companies in Dongguan include DuPont of the United States; Nestle of Switzerland; Philips of the Netherlands; Hoechst of Germany; Thomson of France; Samsung of South Korea; Hitachi, Nippon Steel, Sony, Sumitomo Metal of Japan; Swire Group of the UK; Nokia of Finland, just to name a few.

东莞的本地方言是粤语和客家话,其中樟木头镇完全使用客家话。改革开放之后,中国各地的大量移民进入东莞,普通话成为最通用的语言。

东莞是"粤剧之乡""龙舟之乡"。每年的农历五月初一到十五,石龙和水乡的各个镇、区都会举行龙舟比赛。清溪镇、樟木头镇等的客家山歌表演和比赛也很有名。

The local dialects are Cantonese and Hakka, whereas Zhangmutou Town's people are Hakka speakers only. Since the reform and opening-up, there are a large number of immigrants entering Dongguan from all other areas of China, and Mandarin has become the most common language.

Dongguan is also known as the "Town of Cantonese Opera" and "Town of Dragon Boat". From the first to the fifteenth day of the lunar month of May each year, Shilong and Shuixiang Towns host a dragon boat race. The shows of Hakka folk songs in Qingxi and Zhangmutou Towns are also very popular.

6 广东传统艺术

Guangdong Traditional Arts

采茶戏 Tea-picking Opera

江南的农家女子采茶时，喜欢唱山歌，这种山歌，称为"采茶歌"。采茶戏由采茶歌发展而来，主要流行于江西、湖北、湖南、安徽、福建、广西、广东等地。

粤北采茶戏，以前叫唱花灯、唱花鼓，是在粤北山歌、山调和民间灯彩歌舞的基础上，吸取赣南和湖南益阳的民间艺术而形成的。粤北采茶戏已有 200 多年的历史，主要流行于广东北部客家地区。粤北采茶戏以客家方言演唱，人物安排、情节设计、语言运用轻松活泼、质朴风趣，充满喜剧色彩。

粤北采茶戏一般采用"一唱众和"的形式，也就是台上一名演员演唱，在演员演唱到每句的末尾时，其他演员、乐师和唱"啊嗬""咿哟"等。

粤北采茶戏有生、旦、丑三个行当，以旦、丑为主。旦角表演基本功，包括唱、做、念、舞，具体有步法、指法、梳妆、扇花、手巾等。丑角表演舞蹈动作，如矮子步、扇花步、单袖筒。

粤北采茶戏有传统剧目 300 多个，也有反映现实生活的现代戏，如"女儿上大学"等。粤北采茶戏很受观众的喜爱，并多次获奖。

During tea-picking, farm girls in southern China love to sing mountain folk songs. The folk songs of this type are known as "Tea-picking Songs". Tea-picking Opera originated from Tea-picking Songs and are very popular in Jiangxi, Hubei, Hunan, Anhui, Fujian, Guangxi and Guangdong Provinces.

Yue Bei (northern Guangdong) Tea-picking Opera is known as "Singing Lantern" or "Singing Drum", which is based on the local northern Guangdong mountain folk songs, folk tunes, and lantern dances. It is combined with folk stage art in south of Jiangxi and Yiyang of Hunan, and it has more than 200 years of history and is mainly popular in the Hakka area in northern Guangdong. It is performed and sung in the Hakka dialect. In terms of character, plot design and language use, it is full with a very lively, honest, and humorous comedy style.

Yue Bei Tea-picking Opera is normally in the form of "one singing and more joining ", that is, an actor sings on stage and every time to the end of each stanza, other actors will join in the singing with "ah ho", or "yi yo" or similar phrases like that.

Yue Bei Tea-picking Opera has three roles, namely Sang (male role), Daan (female role) and Cau (clown), but the main roles are Daan and Cau. Daan performs basic skills, including singing, acting, reading, dancing, specifically the footwork, fingering expressions, dressing, fan flower, towel and so on, while Cau performs dance movements, such as dwarf step, fan and flower step, single sleeve.

There are more than 300 traditional repertoires, and there are also some modern drama reflecting current daily life, for example,"Daughter Goes to University". Tea-picking Operas are loved by people and have won numerous awards.

广东音乐 Guangdong Music

广东音乐是中国的传统乐种，流行于珠江三角洲和广府方言区，是优秀的民间传统文化瑰宝；以其轻、柔、华、细、浓的风格和清新流畅、悠扬动听的岭南特色而深受欢迎，遍及中国的大江南北，流行于世界各地。

广东音乐有400多年的历史。现有曲名和乐谱500多首。常用的乐器有高胡、扬琴、秦琴、洞箫、大阮、中胡等，以高胡为主奏乐器，其中"滑指"是广东音乐最有特色的演奏手法。著名的曲目有"步步高""雨打芭蕉""平湖秋月""龙飞凤舞""饿马摇铃"等。

20世纪二三十年代是广东音乐的鼎盛时期，曾被誉为"国乐"。广东音乐音色清脆明亮、节奏清晰明快，被国外誉为"透明音乐"，影响力远远超过中国其他民间音乐形式。在海外，凡是有华人的地方就有广东音乐，广东音乐被称为"乡音"。

6 广东传统艺术
Guangdong Traditional Arts

Guangdong music is a type of traditional Chinese instrumental music and is popular in Pearl River Delta and areas where people speak Cantonese. It is a treasure of folk traditions. The music, in style of light, soft, elegant, slim and rich, is smooth, fresh and melodious; hence very popular all over China and the world.

Guangdong music has more than 400 years of history and has more than 500 well-known pieces. The most common music instruments include Gaohu, Yangqin (dulcimer), Qinqin, Xiao (Chinese vertical bamboo flute), Big Ruan, Zhonghu. Among them Gaohu is the main instrument and the finger style of the "slide figure" is most special in music. The common music tracks are "Bu Bu Gao (Step Step Up)", "Yu Da Ba Jiao (Rain Patteringing Banana Leaves)", "Ping Hu Qiu Yue (Serene Lake with Autumn Moon)", "Long Fei Feng Wu (Flying Dragon and Dancing Phoenix)", and "E Ma Yao Ling (Hungry Horse Shaking Bell)", to name a few.

During the 1920's and 1930's, the peak period of Cantonese music, it was called "the national music". The sound of Guangdong music is crisp and bright, its rhythm is clear and crisp and was praised as the "Transparent Music" abroad. Its popularity is far more than any other folk music forms of China. Wherever there are overseas Chinese, Guangdong music is treated as the "motherland sound".

客家山歌 Hakka Hill Songs

客家山歌是中国民歌体裁中山歌类的一种,它继承了《诗经》[1]的传统风格,受到唐诗和竹枝词[2]的重大影响,同时又吸取了南方各地民歌的优秀成分,至今已有1000多年的历史。客家山歌流行于广东东部、江西南部、福建西部以及台湾北部等地。因为用客家方言演唱,所以叫作"客家山歌"。

按内容划分,客家山歌有劳动歌、劝世歌、行业歌、谜语歌等;按曲调划分,有正板山歌、快板山歌、叠板山歌、号子山歌等;按唱腔划分,有松口原板山歌、梅县山歌、兴宁罗岗山歌、蕉岭长潭山歌、大埔西河山歌等。客家山歌经常使用比兴、双关的手法,语言通俗,朗朗上口,旋律优美。

客家山歌流行的原因有:第一,客家人居住在山区地带,辛苦劳作,通过唱歌来抒发自己的感情;第二,唱山歌正是一种大众化的娱乐形式,简单易行;第三,客家女子和男子一样,长年在山间工作,彼此以唱山歌来传情达意。

---

[1]《诗经》,又叫《诗三百》,是中国第一部诗歌总集,收录自西周初年(公元前1046年)到春秋中叶(公元前476年)五百多年的诗歌305篇。西汉时被奉为儒家经典,开始叫《诗经》,一直沿用至今。

[2] 竹枝词是唐代诗人刘禹锡在古代巴蜀民歌的基础上创造的一种诗体。

Hakka Hill Songs (Folk Songs) are a kind of Chinese folk songs, and the songs are sung in Hakka dialect. Hakka Hill Songs inherited the traditional style from *Shi Jing* (*The Book of Songs*) [①], and are greatly influenced by Tang Poetry, the Zhuzhi lyrics [②], and also by excellent elements from other folk songs in southern China area. Hakka Hill Songs have by now more than 1,000 years of history, and are popular in eastern Guangdong, southern Jiangxi, western Fujian, northern Taiwan and other areas.

Classified by the content, Hakka Hill Songs have work songs, persuasion songs, business songs, and riddle songs. Classified according to tunes, there are Zhengban songs, allegro songs, Dieban folk songs, chant songs and more. Divided by singing techniques, there are Songkou original songs, Meixian songs, Xingning Luogang songs, Jiaoling Changtan songs, Taipo Xihe songs, etc. The Hakka Hill Song is mainly expressed by using the traditional techniques "Bi and Xing" as well as pun, overlapping, and other techniques. It is lively and humorous, easy to understand, and has lovely and elegant tunes.

There are few reasons for Hakka Hill Songs being so popular. First, the Hakka people live and work in mountainous areas, and they sing for expressing their emotions and feelings. Second, singing songs is the easiest and simplest entertainment. Third, folk songs are used to express love between Hakka girls and boys in mountainous area.

---

① *Shi Jing*, also called *The Book of Songs*, was the very first poetry book in China, which collected 305 poems from the West Zhou Dynasty (BC 1046) to the mid-Spring and Autumn Period (BC 476), over a period of more than 500 hundred years. It was honored as classics of Confucian School in the West Han Dynasty and was named as Shi Jing, which has been continually in use to now.

② Zhuzhi lyric was a style of lyrics originated by the poet Liu Yuxi in the Tang Dynasty based on Ba and Shu (Sichuan Province) folk songs.

岭南画派 Lingnan School of Painting

岭南画派是由广东籍画家组成的一个画派，是中国传统国画中的革命派。岭南画派开始于晚清时期，和粤剧、广东音乐合称"岭南三秀"。创始人是高剑父、高奇峰、陈树人，合称"二高一陈"。

岭南画派的特点有：①继承中国国画的传统，在绘画技术上，不用勾勒法，而用"没骨法"①和"撞水撞粉②法"，画作形象逼真；②引入西方绘画的画法，主张写实；③力求创新，以岭南特有的景物为题材。画作富有时代精神和地方特色。

其中高剑父在中国画传统技法的基础上，融合日本和西洋画法，着重写生，擅长用色彩或者水墨进行渲染。他擅长画人物、山水、花鸟，画作笔墨苍劲奔放、充满激情。他还擅长书法，喜欢用鸡毫笔写书法，风格雄厚奇拙。其作品《雨景图》收藏在北京故宫博物院，《鸢尾蜻蜓》收藏在中国美术馆。

---

①"没骨法"指直接用彩色颜料作画，不用墨笔勾勒画作的轮廓。
②"撞水撞粉"：趁颜料还没有干的时候，把清水加在画作上叫"撞水"；把加了白粉的水加在画作上叫"撞粉"。

6 广东传统艺术
Guangdong Traditional Arts

Lingnan School of Painting is composed of a group of Cantonese painters, and it has revolutionarily developed the traditional Chinese painting. It was formed in latter time of the Qing Dynasty (beginning of the 20th Century). It is one of "Lingnan Three Best" together with Cantonese Opera and Guangdong Music. The founders of Lingnan School of Painting were Gao Jianfu, Gao Qifeng, and Chen Shuren, known as "Two Gaos and One Chen".

The distinctive features of Lingnan School of Painting are: First, it inherits techniques from the tradition of Chinese painting and does not use the method of outline, using "mogu" [1] or boneless and "Zhuang Shui and Zhuang Fen [2] (Direct Water and Powder)" techniques instead, which makes the paintings very vivid. Second, it combines Western painting style and techniques, focusing on realistic proposition. Third, it pursues the innovation, and the uniqueness of Lingnan scenery as the main theme. The art works are full of the spirit of the times and local characteristics.

Based on traditional techniques, Gao Jianfu integrated Japanese and Western painting techniques and focused on painting real objects. He was good at using colours and ink to express the theme. He specialized in painting figures, landscapes, flowers and birds, and his works were bold and spirited, full of passion. He was also specialized in calligraphy and liked to use the Ji Hao (Chicken feather) brush pen for calligraphy; his style was solid and unique. His painting *In the Rain* is kept in Beijing Palace Museum, and *Iris Dragonfly* is collected by the National Art Gallery of China.

---

[1] "Mogu Technique" is a painting technique directly using color paint without using brush pen for lines and outlines.

[2] "Zhuang Shui and Zhuang Fen (Direct Water and Powder)" technique is another painting technique. Before the paints become dry, applying clear water to the painting is called Zhuang Shui and adding pigment powder in the water is called Zhuang Fen.

广东文化与社会

高奇峰是高剑父的弟弟,擅长画翎毛、花鸟、走兽,尤其擅长画雄狮、猛禽。山水画、人物画也画得很好,用笔能粗能细,能工能写。工笔画用笔细致入微,写生画水墨淋漓、笔力豪放。其中以写生画最为突出,和他哥哥一样,他也擅长用色彩或者水墨进行渲染。画风工整刚劲、真实清新。

此外,陈树人的画风清新、恬淡、空灵,独树一帜。

6 广东传统艺术
Guangdong Traditional Arts

Gao Qifeng was the younger brother of Gao Jianfu. He was specialized in painting feathers, flowers, birds, animals, especially lions and birds of prey. He was also excellent in painting landscapes and portraits. He paid a lot of attention to details in Gongbi (meticulous) paintings and used ink fluently in Xiesheng (sketching) paintings, with his pen being bold and unconstrained. Like his brother, his Xiesheng painting were outstanding, and he was also good at using colours and ink. His noticeable style is neat, bold, real and simple.

In addition, the unique painting style of Chen Shuren is fresh, tranquil and ethereal.

木偶戏 Puppet Show

木偶戏是用木偶来表演故事的一种戏剧形式。表演的时候,演员在幕后一边操纵木偶,一边配乐演唱。根据木偶形体和操纵技术的不同,分为布袋木偶、提线木偶、杖头木偶、铁线木偶等。

广东高州木偶戏以杖头木偶为主,又称"鬼戏""鬼仔戏",至今已经有400多年的历史。木偶用坚韧的木料制作而成,对木偶进行变形的、夸张的彩绘、装饰。木偶造型精巧,形神兼备,栩栩如生。

高州木偶戏一般由一名演员表演,集唱、做、吹、打于一身。演员不仅能使木偶的头、手、肘、腕、指、腰、腿伸屈自如,而且能使木偶的眼、口开闭。表演中,木偶可开合扇子、穿衣服、戴帽子、倒酒、拿书、写字、拉弓射箭等,一举一动,准确自然。

高州木偶戏在单人木偶(小班)的基础上,又发展出四人班和八人班(中班),十人以上班(大班)。

高州单人木偶多次到北京演出,获得成功。并曾赴法国、德国、中国港澳等地演出,受到各地民众的欢迎。2003年,高州获"中国民族民间艺术(木偶)之乡"的称号。

Puppet show is a theatre performance in which puppet figures are made to move by puppeteers pulling strings or by putting their hands inside them, normally with music or songs. According to the different shapes and manipulation techniques, the puppets can be divided into glove puppets, marionette, rod-top puppets, wire puppets, etc.

Gaozhou puppet show, in Guangdong, mainly uses the rod-top puppets, also known as "ghost show" or "little ghost show" and has a history of over 400 years. The puppets are made of hard wood materials; then painted with exaggerated colours and decorated with costumes, becoming exquisite, vivid and very lifelike.

In Gaozhou puppet show, there is normally only one puppeteer who does all the work including operating the puppets, singing, playing music instruments and drums. The puppeteer can not only control the movement of the puppet's head, hands, elbows, wrists, fingers, waist and legs freely, but also the puppet's mouth and eyes. Puppets can open and close a paper fan, put on clothes or hat, serve wines, hold a book, write words, pull a bow and make many other actions. All the movements are very articulate and natural.

The single puppeteer puppet performance is further expanded to four puppeteers, eight puppeteers and even ten puppeteer groups.

Gaozhou single puppeteer puppet shows have been performed many times in Beijing and all have been very successful. They have also been performed in France, Germany, China's Hong Kong and Macao, and were welcomed and popular. Gaozhou won the title of "Town of Chinese Folk Art (puppet)" in 2003.

粤剧 Yue Opera

粤剧,是广东省地方代表戏曲之一,发源于佛山,同时受到其他剧种的影响,具有岭南文化的特色。

粤剧的表演工艺和京剧一样,分为唱、做、念、打。"唱"指唱功,不同的角色有不同的演唱方式;"做"指做功,也就是身体表演;"念"指念白,念台词;"打"指武打动作。

粤剧的角色行当包括文武生、小生、正印花旦、二帮花旦、丑生、武生。"生"代表男性角色;"旦"代表女性角色;"丑"代表滑稽角色;"武"代表擅长武艺的角色。

粤剧最常见的化妆是"红白脸",把整个脸涂上白色粉底,围绕眼睛和颧骨涂抹红色的胭脂,有时候也涂抹口红。化妆颜色以红、黑、白、蓝、黄为主。红色代表血性忠勇,黑色代表刚忠耿直,白色代表奸恶阴险,蓝色代表狂妄凶猛,黄色代表剽悍干练。

粤剧的服装也很有特点,不同的行当穿不同的戏服,如"小生"饰演文质彬彬的角色,穿长袖,称为文袖;"武生"需要打斗,穿短袖,称为武袖。

据说粤剧剧目有 11000 多个。

Yue Opera (Cantonese Opera) is one of the major local opera genres in Guangdong. It was originally from Foshan area and has been influenced by other opera genres, but it has unique characteristics of the Lingnan culture.

Same as Peking Opera, the types of play include singing, acting, speaking and the martial arts. "Singing" stands for singing skill, and every single role has their own form of singing. "Acting" stands for stage performance with body movements, and "speaking" is for the reading of an actor's lines. Martial arts include performance of both martial arts and acrobatics.

There are a number of types of roles in Yue Opera, which are Man Mou Sang (civilized martial man), Siu Sang (young gentleman), Faa Daan (the first flower of the ball, young belle), Yi Faa Daan (the second flower, supporting female), Cau Sang (male clown), Mou Sang (male warrior role) and many others. "Sang" stands for male actors, "Daan" stands for female actors, "Cau" stands for clowns, and "Mou" stands for warriors.

The most commonly make-up in Yue Opera is "white and red face", an application of white foundation and a red colour around the eyes that fades down to the bottom of cheeks, sometimes also using lipstick. The main colours for make-up are red, black, white, blue and yellow, with red standing for bold, loyal and brave; black for strong and honest; white for wicked and sinister; blue for arrogant and fierce; and yellow for tough and capable.

The costume in Yue Opera is also very special, and each type of play is associated with particular costumes. For example, the role of "Siu Sang" is a gentleman with long sleeves normally, known as "water sleeves of Man"; but "Mou Sang" needs to perform martial arts, so short sleeves are used, which is known as "water sleeves of Mou".

It is said that there are more than 11,000 plays of Yue Opera.

7 广东名胜古迹

Guangdong Historical Sites

陈家祠 Chen Clan Temple

陈家祠，原来叫陈氏书院，是由清朝末期广东省七十二县的陈姓人士共同出资修建的，作为各地的陈氏读书人来广州参加科举考试时的住所，是广东地区保存比较完整的、有代表性的民间宗祠建筑。陈家祠位于广州市中山七路。

陈家祠于清朝光绪十四年(1888年)开始修建，光绪二十年(1894年)建成，占地面积1.5万平方米，建筑面积6400平方米。陈家祠主体建筑为五座三进、九堂六院，以大门、聚贤堂和后座为中轴线，由大小19座建筑组成。各个建筑彼此独立，又通过青云巷、廊等互相联系起来。外围是用青砖砌成的围墙。整体上是一座外封闭、内开放的建筑群体。陈家祠规模宏大，装饰华丽，文物众多。

"聚贤堂"是陈家祠的主殿堂和中心。刚建成时，聚贤堂是陈氏族人集会议事的场所，后来改作宗祠，两边的侧房作为书院。

Chen Clan Temple (Chen Jia Ci), called Chen Clan Academy in the past, was built in the late Qing Dynasty with joint funding from members of the Chen from 72 counties. It was used as a hostel for scholars of Chen Clan in Guangdong area who came to Guangzhou taking part in the imperial examinations. It is a representative of civil ancestral architecture well preserved in Guangdong. Chen Clan Temple is located on Zhongshan Seventh Road, Guangzhou City.

Chen Clan Temple's construction started in the Guangxu fourteenth year (1888) and finished in Guangxu twentieth year (1894) during the Qing Dynasty. It occupies a total area of 15,000 square meters, including the construction area of 6,400 square meters. The main architecture of Chen Clan Temple includes five building groups, three sections, nine halls and six courtyards. The central axis has the main gate, Juxian Hall and Back Building, in total nineteen buildings, and each of them is detached but connected by Qingyun Lane and corridor. The outside walls are made of blue bricks; the style of the building is closed outside and open inside. Chen Clan Temple is vast in territory, beautiful in decoration and contains many cultural relics.

"Juxian Hall" is the main hall and the centre of Chen Clan Temple. In the beginning, it served as the meeting room for Chen families and later became the worship hall and the buildings at both sides were used as study rooms.

陈家祠装饰精巧,堂皇富丽。顶檐、厅堂、院落、廊庑等都有木雕、石雕、砖雕、泥塑、陶塑、铁铸工艺等大大小小的装饰。装饰风格或粗犷豪放,或精致纤巧,各有千秋。特别是祠堂的琉璃瓦脊,刻画着神话传说、古代故事和地方风物,琳琅满目,美不胜收。祠堂前的壁间有六幅大型砖雕,用一块一块雕刻好的青砖连成一体,像画一样展开,每幅砖雕长4米。立体化的砖雕层次清晰,画面内容有神话传说、山水园林、花草树木、飞禽走兽、钟鼎彝铭等。

1959年,经过修缮后的陈家祠改为广东民间工艺馆,1994年改名为广东民间工艺博物馆。1996年被评为"广州十大旅游美景"之首。2002年入选广州"新世纪羊城八景"。2004年被评选为广州市文化名片。

7 广东名胜古迹
Guangdong Historical Sites

Chen Clan Temple is grand and magnificent with delicate decorations. It contains all size of ornaments and decorations, such as wood carvings, stone carvings, brick carvings, clay sculptures, ceramics sculptures, cast-iron crafts which can be seen on roofs, eaves, halls, courtyards and galleries, etc. The decorations have a either rough unconstraint or fine and delicate style, and each has its own character. The especially noticeable markings are the dazzling and beautiful glazed tiles depicted with the myths and legends, ancient stories, and local sceneries. In the intramural located in the front of the temple, there are six large-scale brick carvings displayed like a painting, made of pieces carved blue bricks, and each piece of them is four meters long. The brick carving has a clearly three-dimensional view, and the content includes myths and legends, landscapes, gardens, flowers and trees, bells and inscriptions.

In 1959, Chen Clan Temple was transformed to a type of Guangdong Folk Art Exhibition Hall after repair and redecoration and then renamed again as Guangdong Folk Art Museum in 1994. It was selected as number one among the "Top Ten Guangzhou Tourist Resorts" in 1996, and selected as one of the "Eight Sights of New Century in Guangzhou" in the year 2002. It was also honoured with the title of "Cultural Card of Guangzhou" in 2004.

南海神庙 Temple of Nanhai God

南海神庙，又叫波罗庙，是中国古代海神庙中唯一遗留下来的最完整、规模最大的建筑群，也是广州作为海上丝绸之路起点的重要见证。南海神庙坐落在广东省广州市黄埔区庙头村，修建于隋开皇十四年（公元594年），已有1400多年的历史。

南海神庙具有明代建筑风格，占地面积3万平方米。寺庙入口处有一个"海不扬波"的石牌坊。主体建筑沿中轴线依次递进，包括头门、仪门、礼亭、大殿、昭灵宫。其他建筑都以中轴线为中心，左右对称分布。南海神庙是典型的中国传统庙宇建筑。

7 广东名胜古迹
Guangdong Historical Sites

Temple of Nanhai God (South China Sea God), also known as Boluo Temple, is the only rewaining ancient temple of the Sea God. It is the best preserved temple of its type and size in China and is the witness of Guangzhou being the starting point of the Maritime Silk Road, a route of marine trade. Temple of Nanhai God is located in Miaotou Village, Huangpu District, Guangzhou City, Guangdong Province. It has a history of more than 1,400 years dating back to its construction in the fourteenth year of the reign of Emperor Suikai (594 AD).

Temple of Nanhai God is in the style of the Ming Dynasty architecture and occupies an area of 30,000 square meters. At the front entrance there is a stone arch of "No Wave on Sea". Along the central line of the axis in progression there is a gate, a second gate (Yi Gate), Ceremony Pavilion, Grant Hall and Zhaoling Palace. All other buildings are symmetrically distributed on both sides. Temple of Nanhai God is a typical traditional Chinese temple architecture.

大殿是南海神庙最重要的建筑,是仿明代木结构琉璃瓦歇山顶建筑。屋顶覆盖着绿色的琉璃瓦;中间有双凤翱翔、鳌鱼倒挂等琉璃瓦脊;上面有两条腾飞疾走状的苍龙,两条苍龙正在争夺一颗宝珠。据说双凤代表美丽,鳌鱼代表自由,苍龙代表权力,宝珠代表智慧。大殿内安放着南海之神祝融像,神像连座高3.8米,祝融头戴王冠,身穿龙袍,手拿玉圭,体态丰盈,神情端庄。大殿东侧有一面著名的东汉大铜鼓,铜鼓直径138厘米,高71.4厘米,厚0.4~0.6厘米,是中国现存的三大铜鼓之一,极其珍贵。

海上丝绸之路在中国西汉时开始形成,到隋唐时期达到鼎盛。海上丝绸之路的航线长达1万多千米,扩大了中国在世界上的影响,促进了东西方的文化交流。南海神庙就在这条航线的重要位置上,而且自古就有码头,中外往来的商船经过这个码头时,都会停下来进庙祭祀,祈求一路平安、生意兴隆。南海神庙是中国海上丝绸之路的缩影,具有很高的历史价值和旅游价值。

The Grant Hall is the most important architecture and it mimics wood structure of the Ming Dynasty architecture with its gablet roof of glazed tiles and the roof is laid with green glazed tiles. In the middle there are glazed tile ridges in the shape of double-flying phoenixes or upside-down sea turtles; at the very top, there are two black dragons which look like they are flying up and fighting for a treasure pearl. According to the legend, the double-flying phoenixes represent beauty, and the sea turtles, black dragons and pearl symbolize freedom, power and wisdom respectively. Inside the hall is the Nanhai God (Zhu

Rong) statue. The height of the statue is 3.8 meters including the base. Nanhai God wears a crown and a robe, also holds a Yu Gui (Jade Tablet), and he has a strong body with solemn and dignified expression. Along the east side of the hall is the famous large bronze drum made in the East Han Dynasty, and the diameter of the bronze drum is 138 centimetres, with 71.4 centimetres height and 0.4−0.6 centimetres thickness. It is one of the three remaining drums of this type existing today in China and considered extremely valuable.

The Maritime Silk Road started from the West Han Dynasty and reached its peak around the Sui and Tang Dynasties. The trade journey on the sea was more than 10,000 kilometres, and it has expanded China's influence in the world and promoted cultural exchanges between the East and the West. Temple of Nanhai God is located at the very important location of this trade route. Since ancient times, there has been a harbour, and the merchants from the ships usually stopped here and entered the temple to worship, praying for a safe journey home and a booming business. Temple of Nanhai God is a miniature of China's Maritime Silk Road and has a high historical and tourism value.

南海一号 Sunken Vessel Nanhai No.1

"南海一号"是中国南宋（1127—1279 年）初期在广东省阳江市东平港以南约 20 海里的地方沉没的一艘商船，是目前为止世界上发现的海上沉船中年代最早、船体最大、保存最完整的远洋商船。1987 年，南海一号被发现。2007 年，被整体打捞出水，保存在广东海上丝绸之路博物馆"水晶宫"的沉箱中，在国内外影响很大。

据推算，南海一号是尖头船，从中国驶出，到新加坡等东南亚地区或中东地区进行海外贸易。整艘商船长 30.4 米，宽 9.8 米，高约 4 米，排水量达 600 吨，载重近 800 吨。船舱内保存着 6 万 ~8 万件文物。

7 广东名胜古迹
Guangdong Historical Sites

"Sunken Vessel Nanhai No.1" was a trade ship sunk in the early period of the Song Dynasty (1127–1279). Its last reported location is about 20 nautical miles south of Dongping Port of Yangjiang City in Guangdong Province. It is the oldest, largest, and most intact ocean trade shipwreck which has been discovered in the world. It was found in 1987, and in 2007 the entire wreckage was salvaged and stored in the "Crystal Palace" caisson in the Museum of Guangdong Maritime Silk Road and became well-known at home and abroad.

According to the experts, the ship has a pointed bow. It started from China and went to Southeast Asia including Singapore and even the Middle East for trade business. The ship has a length of 30.4 meters, width of 9.8 meters and height of about 4 meters with water displacement of 600 tons and carrying capacity of about 800 tons. There are 60,000 to 80,000 artifacts preserved in the cabins.

南海一号出水了2000多件完整瓷器，30多个品种，包括德化窑、磁灶窑、景德镇、龙泉窑等宋代著名窑口的精品陶瓷；众多外国的瓷器，如阿拉伯风格的酒壶、大瓷碗；粗大的金手镯、金腰带、金戒指等金器，如长1.7米的鎏金腰带、大口径的鎏金手镯。南海一号出水最多的是铜钱，有上万枚，其中年代最早的是汉代的五铢钱，年代最晚的是宋高宗时期的绍兴元宝。除铁器之外，南海一号还出水了很多用途不明的铜器，如铜环、铜珠等。这一方面表明当时中国的货币是海上丝绸之路的硬通货，另一方面也表明船主非常富有。

南海一号是广东海上丝绸之路的明证，同时也说明，广东文化不仅保留了中原文化，而且还形成了独特的海洋文化。

7 广东名胜古迹
Guangdong Historical Sites

There were more than 2,000 complete porcelain pieces in more than 30 types found from "Sunken Vessel Nanhai No.1", including those from famous kilns like Dehua, Cizao, Jingdezhen and Longquan and some other famous kilns of the Song Dynasty fine ceramics. There were also many foreign porcelains, such as Arab jugs and large bowls, a number of gold wares, such as gold bracelets, gold belts, gold rings, 1.7 meter long gilded belts and large-diameter gilded bracelets. The mostly found were coins, more than 10 thousand pieces ranging from the first five-baht coins in the Han Dynasty to Shaoxing ingot dated from the period of Emperor Gaozong in the Song Dynasty. In addition, some iron wares, copper rings, and bronze beads with unknown uses were found. It proved that Chinese currency was the currency of trade on the Maritime Silk Road and also indicated that the owner was very wealthy.

"Sunken Vessel Nanhai No.1" is the evidence of Guangdong Maritime Silk Road and proves that Guangdong culture is not only retained in Central China culture, but also developed its own unique maritime culture.

广东文化与社会
Cantonese Culture and Society

南华禅寺 Nanhua Temple

南华禅寺是广东省最大的寺庙建筑,是中国佛教著名的寺院之一,是禅宗南宗的主要道场,有"岭南禅林之冠"和"岭南第一山"的称号。据考证,南华禅寺在南朝梁武帝天监元年(公元502年)开始修建,至今已经有1500多年的历史。

南华禅寺位于广东省韶关市曲江区城东南约6千米的曹溪北岸,这里山川秀美、景色宜人。南华禅寺占地总面积约42.5万平方米,主体建筑群总面积1.2万平方米,呈中轴线对称平面布局,阶梯式递进。全寺殿堂飞檐斗拱,多为重檐歇山顶。墙体用青砖灰沙砌成,墙面用琉璃碧瓦铺就。

7 广东名胜古迹
Guangdong Historical Sites

Nanhua Temple is the biggest temple in Guangdong Province, and it is one of the most well-known Buddhist monasteries as well as the main dojo of the Southern Sector of Zen. It is also called "The Crown of Lingnan Buddhist Temple" and "The First Mountain in Lingnan". According to the records, Nanhua Temple was built in the Southern Dynasty, the first year of Liangwu Emperor (502 A.D.), and has more than 1,500 years of history.

Nanhua Temple is located on the northern bank of the Caoxi River, about 6 kilometres south-east to Qujiang County of Shaoguan City, Guangdong Province, nestled within the mountains and rivers with beautiful landscapes. It occupies about 425,000 square meters area in total with about 12,000 square meters of temple ground. It is symmetrically arrayed along the central axis and has steps all the way. All the halls in the temple were built with eaves and brackets, most of which are multi-layered eaves and saddle roof. The halls are made of grey bricks and surfaced with glass glazed green tiles.

唐仪凤二年（公元677年）开始，中国佛教禅宗创始人六祖惠能来这里说法37年。南禅佛法随后在中国广为传播、影响深远。所以南华禅寺有"南禅祖庭"的美誉，与河南省嵩山少林寺并称为禅宗祖庭，在朝鲜、韩国、日本以及欧美等国家和地区有重要影响。

南华禅寺内珍藏着大批珍贵的文物，最著名的是六祖惠能"真身"塑像。惠能是中国佛教禅宗六祖，是中国历史上有重大影响的思想家之一，与代表东方思想的先哲孔子和老子并称为"东方三圣"。记录其言行的《六祖坛经》流传至今，其不腐肉身现存在南华禅寺内。惠能的禅法以定慧为本。他不主张打坐参禅，认为人生来就有佛性，没有烦恼，需要广学多闻，认识自己的本心，在行住坐卧、担水砍柴、吃喝拉撒中也可以领悟佛理，实现顿悟，到达极乐世界。

在南华禅寺的文物中，北齐孝昭帝皇建元年（公元560年）的精美铜佛像年代最早、艺术价值很高的是北宋木雕罗汉像，有360件。

In the second year of Yifeng (677 A.D.) of the Tang Dynasty, the founder of Chinese Buddhism Zen Sect, the 6th Patriarch Huineng, came to the temple and taught Sutra for 37 years. The Southern Sect of Zen then became widely spread in China and very influential in Chinese history. Hence Nanhua Temple gained its reputation of "The Birthplace of the Zen" alongside with Songshan Shaolin Temple in Henan Province and also has major influences abroad in countries and areas including North Korea, South Korea, Japan and countries in Europe and North America.

Nanhua Temple has kept a large number of precious cultural relics. The most famous one is the "Real Body" statue of the 6th Patriarch Huineng. Huineng was the 6th Patriarch of Zen Buddhism in China and also one of the greatest thinkers who had a significant impact on Chinese history, known as "East Trinity", alongside with Confucius and Lao Tzu. *The Book of the 6th Patriarch Platform Sutra* recorded his words and deeds is still published today. His non-carrion body relic is kept in the Nanhua Temple. His practice method of Zen was oriented to Inspirational Wisdom; but did not advocate Zen meditation as he believed a person was born with worry-free and Buddha's nature. One needed only to extensively study the world, to know his or her own heart to become enlightened through daily life such as walking, sitting, resting, carrying water, fetching firewood eating and drinking; hence reaching paradise.

The earliest relics in Nanhua Temple were fine copper Buddha statues dating back to the first year of Huangjian, Xiaozhao Emperor, Northern Qi (560 A.D.). The largest number of relics, reaching 360, is Wooden Arhat statues of the Northern Song Dynasty, which also have significant artistic values.

南越王墓 Nanyue King Tomb

南越王墓是西汉初年南越王国第二代王"文帝"赵眜（公元前137—公元前122年）的陵墓，位于广州市解放北路的象岗山上。1983年6月，南越王墓被发现。挖掘结束后，在原址建立了南越王墓博物馆。

在广东地区，南越王墓是规模最大的一座陵墓，出土文物最多，墓主人身份也最高，是中国境内至今为止发现年代最早的彩绘壁画石室大墓。共出土文物1000多件（套），铜、铁、陶、玉等文物最多。其中"文帝行玺"金印是"皇帝"的印玺，最为珍贵。玉衣是中国汉代特有的丧葬殓服，不同等级的人死后穿不同的玉衣，分为金缕玉衣、银缕玉衣、铜缕玉衣。南越王墓出土的玉衣是丝缕玉衣，玉衣全长1.73米，由2291块玉片组成，用朱红色丝带连接。玉衣头套下的丝囊内装着470颗天然珍珠，珍珠直径0.1~0.4厘米，专家分析是一个丝囊珍珠枕头。"文帝行玺"金印、丝缕玉衣和珍珠枕头，都是中国考古的首次发现。

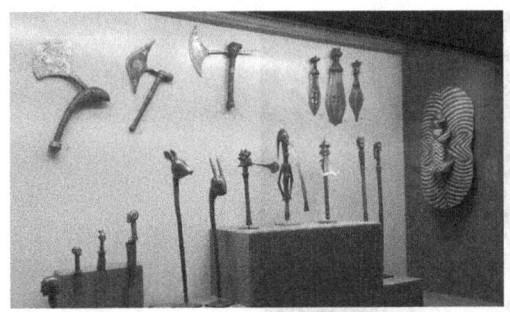

Nanyue King Tomb is the Mausoleum of the second king, Zhao Mei (137-122 B.C.), of Nanyue State in the West Han Dynasty, located at the top of Xianggang Hill on Jiefang North Road, Guangzhou City, Guangdong Province. It was discovered in June 1983, and a museum was built at the same location after the excavation work.

The Nanyue King Tomb has the largest scale, the most excavations, and the highest identity of the owner in Guangdong Province. It has the earliest large stone chamber with colour murals ever found in Chinese tombs. There were more than 1,000 pieces and sets of relics excavated, and most of them were bronze, iron, terra cotta and jade wares. The gold seal, "The Seal of Wen Emperor", is the most precious. Jade burial suits were the typical burial costume in the Han Dynasty, and people of different class levels, after death, would be dressed up in different burial suits. They were normally gold thread burial suits, silver thread burial suits, and copper thread burial suits. However, what was found in the Nanyue King Tomb was a jade gold thread burial suit, which had a length of 1.73 meters and made of 2,291 jade pieces connected with red ribbons. In a silk pocket under the hood of the jade cloth filled 470 natural pearls, with diameters ranging from 0.1 to 0.4 centimetres, and it was said to be a silk pillow filled with pearls by experts. The emperor's seal, the jade burial suit and the pearl pillow, were the first Chinese archaeological discoveries.

南越王墓还出土了最具地方特色的文物——铜提筒。其中有一个船纹铜提筒，高40.7厘米，4只首尾相连的羽人船最引人注目，每条船有5名羽人，他们戴着羽毛做的帽子，光着脚，有的划桨，有的击鼓，有的持兵器在与海盗战斗。船头和船尾分别竖立着一面羽毛做的旗帜。船与船之间还有海龟、水鸟、海鱼等装饰。这个文物是广东海洋文化的见证。

南越王墓还出土了一个白色的银盒。银盒呈扁球形，高12厘米，腹径14.9厘米，重572.6克。银盒内有十盒药丸。经研究，银盒是波斯的产品，银盒里的药丸很可能是阿拉伯药丸。此外，南越王墓还出土了一捆5支原支大象牙，最大的象牙长126厘米。经鉴定，这是通过海上丝绸之路到达广州的非洲象牙。这些文物证明，南越国早期，广州与波斯和非洲东岸进行过海上贸易往来。

南越王墓震惊中国、闻名世界。有人认为，这是中国考古历史上最辉煌的发现之一。

Furthermore, from the Nanyue King Tomb were excavated bronze vessels, relics with local features. Among them, there was an especially noticeable one with a ship pattern, 40.7 centimetres in height. On the body were four ships with a bow connected to a poop carrying feathered figures. In all there were five feathered figures per ship, each wearing a feather hat, bare-footed, and oaring or beating a drum, or holding a weapon battling against pirates. There was a feather banner standing on the bow and poop respectively. There were also decorations of turtles, sea birds, and fishes between the ships. This unique relic is the evidence of Guangdong maritime culture.

Also excavated from the Nanyue King Tomb was a white silver box. The silver box was in sphericity with a height of 12 centimetres and maximum diameter of 14.9 centimetres, and it weighed 572.6 grams which contained 10 boxes of medical pills. After identificatian, it was concluded that the pills were most likely Persian products from Arab countries. In addition, a bunch of 5 large elephant tusks were found. The biggest one was 126 centimetres long. It was identified that they were African elephant tusks which came to Guangzhou via the Maritime Silk Road. All these relics proved that Guangzhou had sea trade and business with Persia and Africa in the period of Nanyue State.

The Nanyue King Tomb caused a sensation in China and became well-known worldwide. It is considered as one of the most magnificent discoveries in Chinese archaeological history.

广东文化与社会
antonese Culture and Society

七星岩摩崖石刻 Qixingyan Moya Stone Carvings

石刻是在石质材料上雕刻出来的各种艺术品。而摩崖石刻是指在天然的石壁上雕刻文字的石刻。七星岩摩崖石刻位于广东省肇庆市城北七星岩风景区内，七星岩有七座石山，崖壁面积不足1.5平方公里，石壁上雕刻着523处从唐朝到现代的石刻。七星岩摩崖石刻是中国南方保存数量最多、最集中的一处石刻群，质量最高，记载着肇庆的地理历史和风土人情。

7 广东名胜古迹
Guangdong Historical Sites

Stone carving means works of art carved out of stone materials and Moya (cliff) Stone Carving for art works with carved text on natural rocks. Qixingyan (Seven Star Crags) Moya Stone Carving is located in Qixingyan Park north to Zhaoqing City, Guangdong Province. There are seven rock hills in the Qixingyan Park, with about 1.5 square kilometres of cliff area and 523 art pieces of carved stones dating from the Tang Dynasty to the modern times. Qixingyan Moya Stone Carvings possess the largest number of the highest quality stone carving groups, and they witness the local history and customs of Zhaoqing.

一千多年以来，到七星岩游览的文人墨客都喜欢在七星岩的石壁上写诗、题字、作画，其中唐朝的有4则，宋朝80则，元朝13则，明朝146则，清朝117则，民国10则，现代109则，年代不明的有44则。七星岩摩崖石刻文体齐备、字体多样、中外兼具。就文体来看，有诗词、歌赋、游记、对联等，其中最多的是诗词、歌赋，仅石室岩内外就有206首，所以有"千年诗廊"的美誉。就文字种类来看，以汉文字为主，兼有藏文和西班牙文。就字体来看，有篆体、隶书、楷书、行书、草书。

在七星岩摩崖石刻群中，年代最久远的是唐朝李邕（公元678—747年）的"端州石室记"。这块石刻高1.07米，宽0.79米，标题、正文、落款一共18行380个字，如今清晰可见的有273个字，尚可辨认的有31个字。落款日期是"开元十五年（公元727年）正月廿五日"。由于石刻中央偏左有一个马蹄形的印记，所以又叫"马蹄碑"。

7 广东名胜古迹
Guangdong Historical Sites

For more than a thousand years, men of letters like poets and painters loved to leave their poems, inscriptions, calligraphic works, or paintings on the cliff rocks, of which 4 were left in the Tang Dynasty, 80 in the Song Dynasty, 13 in the Yuan Dynasty, 146 in the Ming Dynasty, 117 in the Qing Dynasty, 10 in the Republic of China, 109 in recent time and 44 with unknown dates. Qixingyan Moya Stone Carvings have all kinds of calligraphy styles and rich variety of fonts from both China and abroad. Talking about styles, there are poems, lyrics, travel notes, and couplets, but most of them are poems. There are 206 poems around the Stone Cave alone; therefore it is well known as the "Gallery of Millennium Poetry". In terms of types of languages, the majority is in Chinese characters, but there are Tibetan and Spanish too. The styles of the art works include Zhuan (small-seal and big-seal), Li (clerical writing), Kai (regular style), Xing (running script), and Cao (cursive).

Among the stone carving groups in Qixingyan, the oldest one is "Duanzhou Stone Cave", dating back to the Tang Dynasty (678-747 AD) by Li Yong. The piece of stone carving is 1.07 m in height and 0.79 m in width, and there are 18 lines and 386 words in total including title, main text, and signature. By now 273 words are still clearly visible and 31 words recognisable. The date is "25th January, the 15th year of Kaiyuan (727 A.D.)". It is also called "Horseshoe Monument" because there is a horseshoe-shaped mark on the left centre of the stone.

镇海楼 Zhenhai Tower

镇海楼是广东省广州市的标志性建筑之一,坐落在越秀山小蟠龙冈上。因为当时珠江的河道很宽,所以又叫"望海楼"。"海"其实就是珠江,是夸张的说法。又因为一共有5层楼,又叫"五层楼"。镇海楼被誉为"岭南第一胜景"。

1380年,永嘉侯朱亮祖扩建广州城时,把广州北部的城墙扩建到越秀山上,并在山上修建了一座五层楼,镇压住朱元璋所谓的广东"王气",以免除后患。镇海楼曾经五次被毁,五次重建。现在的镇海楼是1928年用木构架改建而成的,为钢筋混凝土结构。镇海楼高28米,歇山式屋顶结构,有复檐五层,红墙绿瓦,雄伟壮观。首层楼面宽31米、深15.77米,山墙厚3.9米,后墙厚3.4米。逐层向上收拢,楼面宽及墙厚尺寸逐步递减,到第五层楼面宽26.4米、深13.67米,山墙厚1.65米,后墙厚1.3米。镇海楼前碑廊有历代流传下来的碑刻,右侧陈列着12门古炮。

清朝以前,镇海楼一直是广州最高的建筑物。登上楼顶,远看,珠江波涛汹涌、水波粼粼;近看则云山层峦叠翠,秀美羊城尽收眼底。几百年以来,文人骚客都喜欢登临镇海楼,或吟咏美景,或抒发志向,或感慨世事,留下了很多著名的诗作。

7 广东名胜古迹
Guangdong Historical Sites

Zhenhai Tower (Tower Controlling the Sea) is one of the landmarks in Guangzhou City, Guangdong Province, located on Little Dragon Hill in Yuexiu Mountain. The tower overlooked the Pearl River which was very wide like the sea at that time, so the building was also called "Sea Watching Tower", but the sea was actually the Pearl River with exaggeration. It was also known as the "Five-storey Building", because it had five storeys. Zhenhai Tower enjoys the reputation of the "Number one most beautiful landscape in Lingnan".

When Guangzhou City was expanded by Duke Yongjia (Zhu Liangzu) in 1380, the north city wall was extended to Yuexiu Mountain. On the top of mountain was built a five-storey tower, which was for suppressing the so-called Guangdong "King Potentiality" claimed by Emperor Zhu Yuanzhang, aiming at eliminating the future threats. Zhenhai Tower had been destroyed and re-built five times in the past. The current tower was re-built with reinforced concrete and replaced the wood frames in 1928. Zhenhai Tower is 28 meters high with saddle roof style and has 5 layers of double-eaves, red walls and green tiles, which looks magnificent. The building's first floor is 31 meters wide and 15.77 meters deep, the thickness of the side walls is 3.9 meters and back walls 3.4 meters. The size of the tower is gradually reduced layer by layer; the width decreased to 26.4 meters, length 13.67 meters, the side wall thickness 1.65 meters and the back wall thickness 1.3 meters on the fifth floor. The steles corridor in front of the tower has a good collection of ancient inscriptions, and on the right hand side 12 ancient cannons are displayed.

Prior to the Qing Dynasty, Zhenhai Tower has been the tallest building in Guangzhou. Watching afar from the top floor, one could see waves of the Pearl River and gleaming water. In the closer range are clouded mountains with a tender green hue, and the most beautiful panoramic view of Guangzhou. For centuries, scholars, artists and poets loved coming to Zhenhai Tower and they composed, chanted, and enjoyed the beautiful landscape, or expressed the aspirations and talked about local current affairs there, which left us with a lot of famous poems.

8 广东建筑
Guangdong Architectures

广东园林 Guangdong Gardens

广东著名的园林包括清晖园、梁园、余荫山房、可园。这四座园林是广东园林的代表。

清晖园原来是顺德黄姓人家的花园,"清晖"的意思是温暖的阳光,比喻父母的恩情。位于广东省顺德区大良镇清晖路,清朝嘉庆五年(1800年)开始修建,1996年扩建成22000多平方米。清晖园的特点有:①实用性。为适应广东潮湿燥热的气候,采用前疏后密、前低后高的布局,显得敞亮通透。②水清木秀,景致优美。碧水、绿树、古墙、漏窗、石山、小桥、曲廊等与亭台楼阁交互融合,造型构筑独具匠心,雕刻、诗画、灰雕等随处可见。

The most well-known gardens in Guangdong are Qinghui Garden, Liangyuan Garden, Yuyinshanfang (Ancestral Beneficence) Garden, and Keyuan Garden, which represent the best gardens in Guangdong.

Qinghui Garden was the garden of Huang's family in Shunde, and the word "Qinghui" means "warm sunshine", a metaphor of the kindness of parents. It is situated on the Qinghui Road of Daliang Town in Shunde District, Guangdong Province. It was built in the fifth year of Jiaqing (1800) during the Qing Dynasty and then expanded to the size of more than 22 thousand square meters in 1996. Qinghui Garden has a couple of special characteristics: ① Practicality. In order to cope with the hot and humid climate in Guangdong, it is designed in a layout of lower and spacious front and compact and higher back and has a feeling of brightness and transparency. ② Beautiful, lovely sceneries with crystal waters and elegant woods. Clear water, green trees, ancient walls, lattice windows, rockworks, petite bridges and zigzag pavilions, which interact with each other, display a splendid and dedicated design with sculptures, poetry and paintings, with stone carvings everywhere.

梁园原来是佛山梁姓人家的宅院,主体建筑位于佛山市松风路先锋古道,主要建筑有"十二石斋""群星草堂""汾江草庐""寒香馆"等。清朝嘉庆、道光年间(1796—1850年)陆续建成,历时50多年,总面积21260平方米。梁园布局精妙,宅第、祠堂与园林浑然一体,尤其以奇峰异石作为重要的造景手法。造园组景不拘一格,树木成荫、繁花似锦、曲水回环、轻盈通透,富有田园风光和地方特色。

余荫山房,又叫余荫园、馀荫山房,原来是番禺邬姓人家的私家花园。位于广州市番禺区南村镇东南角北大街,清朝同治五年(1866年)开始修建,总面积1598平方米。余荫山房是广东四大名园中最小巧,也是原貌保存得最好的古典园林。余荫山房的特点有:①"缩龙成寸"。建筑布局精巧有致,藏而不露。园林内亭、台、楼、阁、堂、轩、桥梁、廊提、石山、碧水等一应俱全,回廊、花窗影壁相互交错,给人以园中有园、景外有景的感觉。②"书香文雅"。诗文、对联、画作等琳琅满目。

8 广东建筑
Guangdong Architectures

Liangyuan Garden was the residential court of the Liang's family in Foshan, Guangdong. The building group is situated at Xianfeng Old Lane, Songfeng Road, Foshan City, and the main buildings include "Shi Er Shi Zhai (Twelve Stone Houses)", "Qun Xing Cao Tang (Stars Cottage)", "Fen Jiang Cao Lu (Fen River Reefs)", "Han Xiang Guan (Hue House)" and others. It was gradually built during the ruling time of Emperors Jiaqing and Daoguang in the Qing Dynasty (1796-1850), in a span of more than 50 years, with a total area of 21,260 square meters. Liangyuan Garden has an exquisite layout with seamless arranged residential mansions, ancestral halls and gardens, especially utilising unique and beautiful rocks as a main theme of creating attractive landscapes. The sceneries are created in styles such as shady trees, varieties of flowers, winding streams, transparent and airy areas, which make the garden rich in rural scenery and local characteristics.

Yuyinshanfang Garden, also called Yuyin Garden, was a private garden of the Wu's family in Panyu. It is situated on North Street, southeast to Nancun Town, Panyu District, Guangzhou City. The construction started in the fifth year of Tongzhi, Qing Dynasty (1866), and it has a total area of 1,598 square meters. Yuyinshanfang Garden is the most exquisite classical garden and the best in preserving the original features among the "Top Four Classical Gardens". It has two outstanding characteristics: ① Miniatures. The compact layout of architecture is exquisite and profound. Within the garden there are pavilions, stages, towers, pagodas, halls, patios, bridges, galleries, rockworks, ponds, with zigzagging corridors and decorated windows intertwining each other, which provides illusions of "gardens inside gardens" and "landscapes outside landscapes". ② Intelligence. Poems, couplets and paintings can be seen everywhere.

可园位于东莞市莞城区博厦村,清朝道光三十年(1850年)开始修建,咸丰八年(1858年)全部建成,总面积2204平方米。整体建筑及围墙都采用水磨青砖,外缘呈三角形。园内有一楼、三桥、五亭、五池、六阁、六台、十五房、十九厅,园林内的建筑大多以"可"字命名。可园的特点有:①四通八达。园林充分运用孙子兵法,整个园林共有130多个出入口,108条柱栋,布局犹如八阵图,在园里行走,非常容易迷路。②小巧雅致。虽然整个园林偏于武略,但局部都具有浓厚的诗情画意。

Keyuan Garden is situated at Bosha Community, Guancheng District in Dongguan City. It began construction in the thirtieth year of Daoguang (1850), and was completed in the eighth year of Xianfeng (1858) in the Qing Dynasty, with an area of 2,204 square meters. Double mill grey clay bricks were used for all buildings and walls, and the periphery of the garden was designed in a triangular shape. There is one tower, three bridges, five pavilions, five ponds, six courtyards, six stages, fifteen houses, and nineteen halls, and most of them are named starting with "Ke", a Chinese character. The special features of Keyuan Garden include: ① Extensions in all directions. The whole garden was designed using the "Art of War" style by Sun Tzu and there are more than 130 entrances and exits, 108 pillars, in a Ba Zhen (eight mazes) layout, and thus it can be quite easy got lost while walking in the garden. ② Petite and elegant. It was built with the elements of Art of War, but it had a profound romantic atmosphere overall.

广州塔 Canton Tower

广州塔,俗称小蛮腰、海心塔、广州新电视塔,2009年9月建成,其中塔身主体高450米,天线桅杆高150米,总高度600米,是广州市的新地标。位于广州市海珠区赤岗塔附近,距离珠江南岸125米。

广州塔塔身是椭圆形的渐变网格结构,由两个向上旋转的椭圆形钢外壳形成,一个在基础平面上,一个在假想的450米高的平面上,两个椭圆各自扭转135°,两个扭转的椭圆在腰部收缩变细。底部的格子式结构比较疏松,腰部比较密集,呈现"纤纤细腰"的状态。再向上,格子式结构放开,由逐渐变细的管状结构柱支撑。顶部的结构更加开放,产生透明的效果,可供远望。塔身整体网状的漏风空洞可以有效减少塔身的笨重感和风荷载。远远望去,广州塔好像一个扭身回看珠江的少女。塔身采用特一级抗震设计,可以抵御烈度高达7.8级的地震和12级的台风。广州塔设计使用年限超过100年。

广州塔是亚洲最高建筑之一,具有观光、发射、展示、游览等功能。同时拥有世界上最高的旋转餐厅、4D影院、横向摩天轮和最长的空中云梯。广州塔曾为2010年第16届广州亚洲运动会提供转播服务。

8 广东建筑
Guangdong Architectures

Canton Tower, also called "Slim Waist", Haixin Tower and Guangzhou TV & Sightseeing Tower, became operational in September 2009. The height of the main tower is 450 metres with an additional antenna height of 150 metres, which makes it 600 metres high in total and it is the newest landmark of Guangzhou City. It is situated near Chigang Tower in Haizhu District, only 125 metres away from the south bank of Pearl River.

The main body of the tower has an oval-shaped structure with curly meshes, which consists of two upward spiral oval-shaped steel shells, one on the foundation ground and the other at an imaginary high platform of the 450 metres. Both ovals twist 135 degrees and the twisted ovals are narrowed down to the waist. At the bottom, the lattice structure is spacious but in the middle section it becomes more compact, resembling a "slender waist". Further up, the tower has a more opened-up lattice structure supported by tapered tabular columns. Towards the top, the structure becomes even more open, providing transparent effects, an ideal spot for overlooking the surroundings. The meshed holes of the whole tower can effectively reduce the tower weight and relief wind load. Seeing the tower from a distance, it resembles a maiden looking back at the Pearl River. The tower uses special levels of seismic design techniques so it can withstand up to 7.8 magnitude earthquake and grade 12 typhoon. The design service life of the tower is more than 100 years.

Canton Tower is one of the highest architectures in Asia, and it provides functions ranging from sightseeing, radio and television transmissions, exhibitions to tourism attraction. It also has the tallest rotating restaurant, 4D cinema and ferris wheel and longest skywalks in the world. Canton Tower provided transmission services in 2010 for the 16th Asian Games.

怀圣寺 Huaisheng Mosque

怀圣寺是中国现存最古老、最有特色的清真寺建筑,是中国四大古代清真寺之一。唐高祖武德年间(公元618—626年),受伊斯兰教创始人穆罕默德派遣,艾比·宛葛素来中国传教,并在唐贞观初年(公元627年)经由海上丝绸之路到达广州。同年,艾比·宛葛素和居住在广州的阿拉伯人捐资修建了这座清真寺。为了纪念圣人穆罕默德,取名"怀圣"。

怀圣寺位于广东省广州市越秀区光塔路56号。主轴线上依次建有三道门、看月楼、礼拜殿和藏经阁。礼拜殿在院庭的正面,是3间带有围廊、歇山重檐绿琉璃和斗拱的古典式阿拉伯风格建筑。

Huaisheng Mosque is the oldest and the most distinctive mosque, and it is one of four ancient mosques in China. During Gaozu Wude years (618-626 A.D.) of the Tang Dynasty, sent by Islamic prophet, Mohammed, Abi Waqqas came to China as a missioner and reached Guangzhou in the first year of Zhenguan(A.D. 627), Tang Dynasty, via the Maritime Silk Road. In that same year, Abi Waqqas and other Arab residences in Guangzhou together donated and built the mosque. They named the mosque "Huaisheng (remember the sage)" to commemorate Mohammed.

Huaisheng Mosque is situated at No.56 Guangta Road, Yuexiu District, Guangzhou City, Guangdong Province. It was built along the main axis of Sandao Gate, Kanyue (Watching the Moon) Tower, Worship Grant Hall and Depositary of Islam Texts. The Worship Grant Hall is at the front of the courtyard, and there are three ancient Arab style buildings with corridors including multi-layered eaves with green glazed glass and brackets.

教徒在诵经时，经常在塔顶用阿拉伯语呼喊"邦卡"，"邦"与粤语的"光"谐音，而且这座塔位于珠江边上，唐朝时，到了晚上，教徒会在塔顶悬挂灯火为来往的船只导航，所以叫作"光塔"，怀圣寺也因此又名光塔寺。光塔高36.3米，用青砖砌成，表面涂有灰沙，塔的底部为圆形。塔身呈圆筒状，向上逐步收拢。塔身开有长方形的小孔，用来采光。塔内设有两个螺旋形的楼梯，楼梯绕着塔心盘旋而上，分别通到塔顶。塔的顶部原来有一只金鸡，可以随风旋转，标志风向，明朝初期被飓风吹落，1934年重修时改砌成尖顶。

中国传统的砖砌佛塔，一般都是方形或转筒形，用木梯或者木楼板上下。后来才使用八角形及砖磴道的砌法，但是砌工简单，远远不如光塔的圆形双楼道的技术精巧。专家研究认为，这种古老的使用砖磴道盘旋而上的圆形砖塔在中国古代建筑中非常罕见。怀圣寺的磴道技术影响并提高了中国砖砌佛塔的建筑技术，是中国工程技术史上的一件大事。

8 广东建筑
Guangdong Architectures

During worship services, the followers often shouted from the roof tops in Arabic "Bang Ka". "Bang" sounds like "Guang" (light) in Cantonese, so the Huaisheng Mosque was also called "Light Tower". Another reason for the name is that the mosque is located at the bank of the Pearl River, and in the evenings during the Tang Dynasty the followers used to hang lights to guide approaching ships. The Light Tower is 36.3 metres in height, built with blue bricks coated with sand lime, and the bottom is in a circular shape. The body of the tower gradually tapers upward. On the tower, there are a number of opened rectangular holes for lighting purposes. Inside the tower, there are two spiral staircases through the centre of the tower going upward. At the top of the tower stood a golden rooster vane sometime ago, rotatable with the wind, for indicating wind directions. It was blown down by a hurricane during the Ming Dynasty. However, the top was rebuilt to a steeple design in 1934.

A traditional Chinese brick Buddha tower was normally built in square or cylinder shapes with wooden stairs or ladders. Later octagon towers with brick stairs were adopted, but the technique of laying bricks was much simpler than the delicate technique of cylinder twin-stairs used in the Light Tower. According to experts, this type of ancient circular brick tower, with spiral and brick stairs, is rarely seen in Chinese ancient architecture. The construction technique of the Huaisheng Mosque greatly influenced and improved architecture technology in Chinese brick Buddha towers, and it was an important evolution in the Chinese history of engineering and technology.

开平碉楼 Kaiping Diaolous

开平碉楼位于广东省开平市境内。明朝（1368—1644年）以来，广东省开平一带社会治安混乱，洪涝灾害严重。后来，为了躲避灾祸，当地民众被迫修建碉楼。20世纪二三十年代，开平修建了很多碉楼。开平碉楼是中国乡土建筑的一个特殊类型，具有古希腊、古罗马、伊斯兰等多种风格。

开平碉楼为多层塔楼式建筑，比一般的民居高得多，这样有利于居高临下地进行防御。碉楼的墙体厚实坚固，可以防止匪盗凿墙或者火攻。

碉楼的窗户很小，设有铁栅和铁板窗门。碉楼上部的四角建有角堡，角堡内设有向前和向下的射击孔。碉楼的各层墙上也设有射击孔。

开平碉楼的顶部最有特点，有一百多种造型，比较美观的有中国式屋顶、中西混合式屋顶、古罗马式山花顶、穹顶、美国城堡式屋顶、欧美别墅式房顶、庭院式阳台顶等。

Kaiping Diaolous (fortified towers) are situated in Kaiping City, Guangdong Province. Since the Ming Dynasty (1368-1644), there had been frequent social disorders and natural disasters in the Kaiping area of Guangdong, so the people built fortified towers to defend themselves. During the 1920s and 1930s, a lot of fortified towers were built in Kaiping, which are regarded as a special type of Chinese vernacular architecture with combined styles from ancient Greek, Roman and Islam.

Kaiping Diaolous are multi-storey towers like buildings but much higher than common seen residential buildings, and have a great advantage during battles from higher positions. The tower has thick and solid walls to defend against digging at the wall or attack using fire by bandits. The windows are very small, installed with metal bars and doors. On the tower top around the four corners are forts which contain shooting holes with forward and downward angles, on each floor with many shooting holes along the walls.

The most special part of the towers is the roof. There are hundreds of types. The Chinese style, Chinese-Western mixed style, ancient Roman style, arched roof, American fort roof, European-American houses and garden balcony are among the beautiful designs.

开平碉楼有很多种类型。按建筑材料可以分为石楼、夯土楼、青砖楼、混凝土楼。按使用功能可以分为众楼、居楼、更楼。众楼造型简单,结构封闭,外部装饰少,防卫性强。由全村或者几户人家共同出资修建在村子后部,每户人家一个房间。众楼出现的时间最早,现存470座左右。居楼楼体高大,空间开敞,兼有防卫和居住的功能。由富有人家独资修建在村子后部,生活设施完善,外观华美,是村落的标志。居楼数量最多,现存1100多座。更楼用以瞭望,一般修建在村口或者村外的山冈上、河岸边,一般都装有探照灯和报警器。更楼出现的时间最晚,现存200多座。

开平碉楼是广东文化主动接受外来文化的历史见证,是中国华侨文化的杰出代表。2007年,广东"开平碉楼与村落"被列入"世界遗产名录"。

There are various types of Kaiping Diaolous. If classified by building materials, there are stone towers, rammed earth towers, brick towers and even concrete towers. If classified by functions, they can be common, private, and watching towers. The common towers are simple with closed structure. They were built together by a number of families, one room per family; they are normally situated on the back side of a village. The common towers are known earliest, and currently there are around 470 towers. The private towers are normally big and tall, spacious with functionalities for both living and defending. They belonged to rich families and had all kinds of facilities, which were beautiful and treated as a landmark of a village. The total in existence of the private Towers now are more than 1,100. The watching towers were used for alerting and normally built at the entrance of a village or on top of a hill or by a river bank. They were normally equipped with alarm and lighting systems. They were built much later than the other two types of towers. At present, there are more than 200 such kinds of towers.

Kaiping Diaolous are the evidences of Guangdong proactively absorbing foreign cultures, and they are also good examples of overseas Chinese culture in architecture. In 2007, "Kaiping Diaolous and Villages" were included in the "World Heritage List".

骑楼 Riding Buildings

骑楼是商业和住宅合为一体的建筑，是指楼房骑跨人行道而建、在马路边互相连接而形成的可供自由步行的长廊及其楼房。骑楼长达几百米，甚至上千米，包括楼顶、楼身、骑楼底。骑楼最早出现在2000多年前的古希腊，后来在欧洲流行，近代传到世界各地。在中国东南沿海的城镇比较常见。

广东骑楼融合西方古代建筑的精神和中国南方传统文化的精髓，因地制宜发展起来。骑楼跨出街面，既扩大了居住面积，又可以遮风挡雨防日晒，特别适合广东潮湿燥热的气候环境，方便顾客自由通行、选购商品。楼下做商铺，楼上住人，非常实用。

8 广东建筑
Guangdong Architectures

Qilou (Riding Building) is a type of architecture combined business and residential uses, and it normally refers to buildings along streets and connected together providing a long walking path. A Qilou can be as long as a few hundred or even a few thousand meters, including the ground floor, main building, and roof. The earliest Riding Buildings were seen in ancient Greece over 2,000 years ago which became popular in Europe and then spread all over the world. They are more commonly seen along the southeast coastal areas of China.

Qilou in Guangdong combined the style of ancient Western architecture and the essence of southern China traditional culture, gradually adopted according to the local environment. Qilou is extended to street space; in this way the living area is enlarged, and it can provide shelter against rain and sunburn, especially suitable for the Guangdong area with its damp and hot climate. It can also provide convenience to pedestrians and shoppers. It has a great business advantage since the ground floor can be used as shops and the upstairs as living quarters.

广州骑楼是粤派骑楼的代表,保存完整,有仿哥特式、南洋式、古罗马券廊式、仿巴洛克式、中国传统式和现代式等样式。其中仿哥特式有广州市北京路新华书店,南洋式有文明路186号,古罗马券廊式有新华大酒店,仿巴洛克式有万福路114号,中国传统式有德政南路139号。此外,第十甫路、上下九路、中山路、解放路、人民南路、一德路等地的骑楼比较多。西濠口一带的骑楼则最宏伟。新亚酒店、南方大厦、爱群大厦等是广州初期骑楼的代表。20世纪60年代以后,广州新建的商业街区很少采用骑楼这种建筑形式。

8 广东建筑
Guangdong Architectures

Guangzhou's Riding Buildings are the typical representatives of Riding Buildings in Guangdong and they are well preserved in various forms. These typical forms include Gothic-like style, Nanyang (Southeast Asia) style, Roman gallery-style, Baroque-like style, modern and traditional Chinese style. A good example of Gothic-like style is the Xinhua Bookstore on Beijing Road; No.186 on Wenming Road is Nanyang style. Xinhua Hotel is Roman gallery-style; No.114 on Wanfu Road is Baroque-like style; No.139 on Dezheng Road South is traditional Chinese style. There are a lot of Riding Buildings in the area of Dishifu Road, Shangxiajiu Road, Zhongshan Road, Jiefang Road, Renmin South Road and Yide Road. Riding Buildings in Xihaokou are the most magnificent. New Asia Hotel, Nanfang Shopping Mall and Aiqun Building are the good examples of the earliest Riding Buildings in Guangzhou. After the 1960s, the new commercial districts of Guangzhou rarely selected this design of buildings.

圣心大教堂 Sacred Heart Cathedral

圣心大教堂是广州最大的天主教堂,是中国现存最宏伟、最有特色的双尖塔哥特式建筑之一,是东南亚地区最大的天主教石结构建筑,也是全世界四座全石结构的哥特式教堂建筑之一,有"远东巴黎圣母院"的美誉。圣心大教堂于1863年6月18日圣心瞻礼日举行奠基典礼,所以取名"圣心大教堂"。因为教堂的全部墙壁和柱子都是用花岗岩砌成,所以又叫"石室""石室耶稣圣心堂""石室天主教堂"。

圣心大教堂位于广东省广州市一德路。1863年开始修建,1888年建成,至今已有120多年的历史。

8 广东建筑
Guangdong Architectures

The Sacred Heart Cathedral is the largest Catholic Church in Guangzhou. It is the biggest and most magnificent cathedral currently existing in China and features twin towers in a Gothic style. The cathedral is also the biggest solid masonry catholic architecture in Southeast Asia and has a nickname— "Oriental Notre Dame de Paris". It got this name due to its groundbreaking ceremony held on June 18th, 1863, the day of the Sacred Heart Feast. Because all of its walls and pillars are made of granite, it is also called "Stone House", "Stone House Sacred Heart of Jesus", and "Stone House Catholic Church".

The Sacred Heart Cathedral is located on Yide Road in Guangzhou. It has more than 120 years of history with construction beginning from 1863 and completed in 1888.

圣心大教堂具有哥特式教堂所有建筑元素，是一座地地道道的欧洲中世纪天主教堂。正面看去，教堂呈典型的左右三段式和上下三段式格局，基座是三座尖形拱门，中间的大门最大，左右门对称。这三座门及东西两侧的横门都是层层叠叠的尖券门，具有很强的透视效果。

教堂内部左右两侧分别由10根巨型石柱支撑着尖拱，教堂内部和外观一样，有一种向上的升腾感。教堂内顶中间最高，两侧稍低，呈起伏状。因为石柱的排列和教堂内顶的尖拱结构，从大门向祭坛方向望去，整个大堂显得庄重、肃穆，有一种无限延伸的感觉。教堂内正面、东面、西面各有直径7米的圆形玫瑰花窗，镶嵌着深红色、深蓝色、黄色和紫色的玻璃，玻璃窗上绘有圣经故事。

教堂的外顶部是两座高耸的尖顶石塔，象征升向天堂，皈依天主。石塔中间西侧是一座大时钟，东侧是一座大钟楼，装有四个大铜钟。

The Sacred Heart Cathedral has all the architecture features of Gothic Cathedral and is a typical Medieval Europe Catholic Church. From the front, one can see a typical layout of three-sections from left to right, and three-layers from bottom to top. There are three tapered arches, with the biggest one at the middle and one at each side symmetrically. These three arches and two side gates are all types of Pointed Arch Gates bearing a strong perspective effect.

Inside the church there are 10 huge pillars on each side supporting the ceiling arch; one can have a sense of ascending from both inside and outside of the church. The highest point of the hall is the middle of the arch, slightly lower at each side, and up and down. Due to the array of giant pillars and inside pointed arch ceiling, the hall shows an extensional look of sacredness and solemnity if observed from the main gate to altar. On the walls of east, west and north, there are 7-metre diameter circular windows in rose leaf shapes, mounted with red, blue, yellow and purple glasses depicting Bible stories.

Standing on the roof of the church are two high steeple stone towers which symbolize rising to the heaven, being converted to God. In the west side of the middle tower there is a huge clock and on the east side is a big bell tower with four bronze bells inside.

围龙屋 Round-dragon Houses

围龙屋是广东三大民系之一的客家民系最有代表性的建筑。除此之外,客家民居建筑还有圆寨、走马楼、四角楼等。客家围龙屋与北京的"四合院"、陕西的"窑洞"、广西的"杆栏式"和云南的"一颗印"合称中国最具乡土风情的五大传统住宅建筑。客家人的祖先原来是中原的汉族人,因为战乱、灾荒等原因而迁移到江西、广东、福建交界的山区。定居后,他们保留了中原民宅的传统风格,并有较大的创新和发展。

围龙屋的整体布局是一个大圆形,远远望去,好像一个太极图。

围龙屋前半部是一个半月形的池塘,后半部为半月形的房舍建筑。两个半部的接合部位由一个长方形的空地隔开,夯实铺平的空地叫"禾坪",是客家人活动或晾晒谷物的地方。"禾坪"与池塘的连接处用石头砌起一堵石墙。池塘主要用来放养鱼虾、浇灌菜地、蓄水防旱防火。

8 广东建筑
Guangdong Architectures

Round-dragon House is the most represented architecture of the Hakka people who are one of the three main sub-cultures in Guangdong, China. In addition to Round-dragon House, there are other types of Hakka residential buildings, like Yuan Zhai (Circular Village), Zouma Lou, Sijiao Lou (Four Corner Tower), just to name a few. Hakka's Round-dragon House is one of five main Chinese countryside residential architectures, and the other four are "Si He Yuan"(Dwelling Compounds or Quadrangles) in Beijing, "Yao Dong" (Cave House) in Shanxi, "Lan Gan Shi" in Guangxi and "Yi Ke Yin" in Yunnan. Hakka ancestors were originally Han Chinese from Central China, who migrated to boundary mountain areas of Jiangxi, Guangdong and Fujian Provinces because of wars and famines. After resettling down, they kept the style of the ancient Central Chinese traditional architectures, but greatly innovated and created new types of buildings.

The overall layout of the Round-dragon House is a large circle and it looks like a Tai Chi symbol from a distance.

The front half of the Round-dragon House is a crescent shaped fish pond and the back half are residential houses which is also in a crescent shape. In between the two halves is a rectangle plot which is flat and solid, named "He Ping" (crop floor). This serves as common areas for daily activities of the Hakka people and especially for drying grains. There is normally a wall built with stone between the "He Ping" and the pond. The main uses of the pond are raising fish and prawns, irrigating vegetable fields, and preserving water in the event of drought and fire.

房舍建筑的正中是方形的主体建筑,有"三栋二横"一围层和"三栋四横"二围层。最小的围龙屋的建筑面积可达1000平方米,大的上万平方米。有的大围龙屋居住着上百户人家,几百口人。"三栋二横"一围屋比较多,有上、中、下三个厅,各个厅之间都有一个天井,天井用木制的屏风隔开,屏风可打开可关闭。厅堂左右有南北厅、上下廊厕、花厅、厢房、书斋、客厅、居室等。整个围龙屋的结构为前低后高,这样有利于采光、通风、排水、排污。

8 广东建筑
Guangdong Architectures

The middle square of the house is the main building which can be in the style of either "three-files and two-rows" in single circle or "three-files and four-rows" within double circles. The floor area of a small scale Round-dragon House can be a thousand square meters, but the bigger ones can be larger than ten thousand square meters. Some large Round-dragon Houses are big enough for a little more than a hundred families and a few hundred people. The most commonly seen type is the "three-files and two-rows" in a single circle and there are three units: upper, middle and lower, each having its own patio courtyard which is segregated by wooden screens and the screens can be opened or closed. Inside a unit, there are southern and northern halls, corridors and toilets, living rooms, side rooms, study rooms, reception rooms, and bedrooms. Round-dragon House has a structure of lower in the front and higher at the back and in this way it is ideal for lighting, ventilation, drainage and sewage.

西关大屋 Xiguan Houses

清朝（1636—1911年）末期，广东的豪门富商在广州城西"西关角"一带（即现在的荔湾区）修建富有广东地方特色的传统民居，这就是西关大屋。

西关大屋按中原传统的正堂屋形式进行布局。典型平面是三间两廊，左右对称，中间为主要厅堂。中轴线由前而后、由南而北，依次为门廊、门厅（门官厅）、轿厅（茶厅）、正厅（大厅或神厅）、头房（长辈房）、天井、二厅（饭厅）、二房（尾房）。正厅是西关大屋的主体建筑，面积最大、屋脊最高，为红栋（主梁涂红漆）黑桷（木角涂黑漆）白瓦（衬瓦涂成白色）。屋顶装有玻璃瓦，使大厅显得更加宽敞明亮。

Xiguan House is one of the Cantonese local styles of traditional residential houses, situated in the area of "Xiguan Corner" (Liwan District today), Guangzhou, and built by wealthy businessmen in the late Qing Dynasty (1636-1911).

The style of Xiguan House follows the traditional layout of Central China classical houses. The typical floor plan consists of three rooms and two corridors, symmetrical with the main hall in the centre. Along the main axis from south to north there is a gate, gate hall, reception room (tea hall), the main hall, master bedroom, courtyard, the second hall (dinning room), and the second bedroom (the back room). The main hall is the main building which is the biggest and tallest and built with red pillars, black rafters and white tiles. Some glass tiles are used on the roof, which makes the hall spacious and bright.

西关大屋大多采用砖木结构，青砖石脚，正门用花岗石装嵌。室内装饰有木石砖雕、陶塑灰塑、壁画石景、满洲窗、刻彩图案、红木家具、木雕花饰、槛窗等。其中最有特色的是满洲窗，满洲窗是正方形的窗格，用五光十色的玻璃镶嵌而成，华美辉煌。

现存的西关大屋只有小画舫斋。小画舫斋于清朝光绪壬寅年（1902年）建成，是一座环形园林式的西关大屋，中间是花园，四周是楼房。花园花木秀丽，楼房精美雅致。最有特色的西关大屋是李文田探花第，现在仅存的只有探花书轩。

Most of the Xiguan Houses are made of wood and bricks, footed with blue stones, and embedded or decorated on the main gate with granite. Inside the houses there are commonly wood carvings, stone and brick cravings, pottery and plaster sculptures, wall paintings, and rock formations with Manchurian-style windows, colour picture engraved cases, mahogany furniture, floral wood decorations, window sills and much more. The Manchurian-style windows are most interesting which are square shaped and embedded with colourful glass making them beautiful and magnificent.

One of the few surviving Xiguan Houses is the "Xiao Huafang Zhai" (Little Painted-boat House). It was built in the Ren-Yin year (1902) of Emperor Guangxu during the Qing Dynasty and is a circular house with a garden. The garden is in the centre and surrounded by the buildings. The trees and flowers in the garden are beautiful, making the buildings exquisite and elegant. The most distinctive Xiguan House is "Li Wentian Tanhua Di (house)", however, only the Tanhua Library has survived.

中山纪念堂 Sun Yat-sen Memorial Hall

中山纪念堂是一座八角形宫殿式建筑,是广东省广州市近代著名的建筑,位于越秀山南麓的东风中路。

中山纪念堂是为纪念孙中山先生而修建的,1929年1月动工,1931年11月建成,总建筑面积3700多平方米,高49米。原址是孙中山1921年在广州出任临时大总统时的总统府。纪念堂内是一个近似圆形的大会堂,大会堂直径71米,分上、下两层,一共有4700多个座位。四周的墙壁中隐藏着四根大柱子,柱子支撑着四个跨度达30米的大型钢桁架,构成一个巨大的拱形屋顶。拱形屋顶托起八个主桁架,再承托起八角形的堂顶。屋顶外部全部采用蓝色琉璃瓦。会堂式建筑将中国传统宫殿式建筑和西方钢筋混凝土结构结合起来,开创了中西建筑融合的新起点。

8 广东建筑
Guangdong Architectures

Sun Yat-sen Memorial Hall (Zhongshan Jiniantang) is an octagonal palace-style building and a famous modern architecture which is located on Dongfeng Middle Road, southern side of Yuexiu Mountain, Guangzhou City, Guangdong Province.

Sun Yat-sen Memorial Hall was built to commemorate Dr. Sun Yat-sen. The construction started in January 1929 and was completed in November 1931. Its total construction area is 3,700 square meters, and its height is 49 meters. The original site was the presidential palace of Sun Yat-sen as the provisional president of Republic of China in 1921. The Memorial Hall has a roughly circular hall inside, with a diameter of 71 metres, of which there is a lower layer and a upper one housing 4,700 seats in total. Inside the walls are four large hidden pillars which support four large steel trusses with a span of 30-meter, and this constitutes a huge arched ceiling and the ceiling supports eight main arched roof trusses that in turn then support the octagonal roof of the hall. The roof structure all consists of blue glazed tiles. The design of the hall combines traditional Chinese palace architecture with Western-style buildings which were adapted to reinforced concrete structures. It was a new starting point for the integration of Chinese and Western architecture design and style.

纪念堂前矗立着5米高的孙中山铜像。沿着铜像往正门走,有两段台阶,分别有九级和五级。中国古代通常以"九"和"五"象征帝王的权威,称为"九五之尊"①。纪念堂主体建筑上的每一根圆柱柱头都装饰有"￥"形图案,和人民币的符号"￥"一样。这个符号其实是"羊"字,与广州"五羊献穗"的传说有关,表达羊城人民对孙中山的怀念之情。

---

①九五之尊:古代中国人认为,"九"是最大的阳数(奇数),有最尊贵的意思;"五"处在阳数中间,有调和的意思。这两个数字组合在一起,有"既尊贵又和谐"之意。

8 广东建筑
Guangdong Architectures

In front of the Memorial Hall stands a 5-meter high bronze statue of Sun Yat-sen. Walking pass the statue towards the main entrance, there are two layers of steps with nine and five steps respectively. In ancient China, the numbers of nine and five usually symbolize the authority of the emperor, known as the "Nine and Five for Royalty"[①]. On the stigma of each pillar of the Memorial Hall is decorated with a pattern of "¥", which is the same as the symbol of Chinese currency "yuan" (¥). This symbol is actually one of the Chinese characters "Yang (Goat)" which has originated from the legend of "Five Goats Gave Grains", expressing Cantonese emotions to Sun Yat-sen.

---

① "Nine and Five for Royalty": In ancient time, Chinese thought the largest single odd number "nine" meant royalty, and the middle odd number "five" meant harmony. The combination of these two numbers represents both royalty and harmony.

9 广东工艺美术
Guangdong Arts and Crafts

端砚 Duan Inkstones

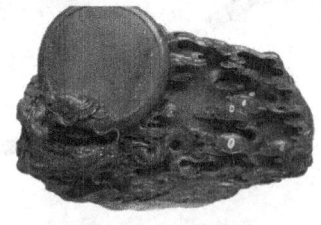

砚，又叫"砚台"。用砚研墨，用笔蘸墨，在纸上写字，笔、墨、纸、砚密不可分，合称为"文房四宝"。中国有"四大名砚"的说法，也就是端砚、歙砚、洮砚、红丝砚，其中端砚最有名。端砚石出产在广东省肇庆市。

自古以来，端砚就十分名贵，原因包括：①端砚石来之不易。端砚石产在水里，开采不容易。目前，出产端砚石的坑道几乎枯竭，所以，所有坑道都已经不允许挖掘。②端砚石质地坚实、润滑、细腻，用端砚研墨不滞，发墨快，研出的墨汁细滑，书写流畅不会损坏毛笔，字迹颜色经久不变。③端砚"有眼"。"眼"就是砚台上的石纹，如"鹦哥眼""鹅哥眼"等。研磨写字时好像有眼睛在注视，增添了情趣。④端砚的制作工序十分繁杂。主要有采石、维料、制璞、雕刻、磨光、配盒等。

端砚具有很高的艺术价值和收藏价值，古代一般作为朝廷的贡品。一般认为，白色的端砚最好，青色次之，紫色最差。世界上最大的端砚是"端溪九龙砚"，长4.6米，宽3.15米，厚0.45米，重13.8吨，被誉为"中华之最"，收藏于肇庆市端茗砚雕工艺厂内。

9 广东工艺美术
Guangdong Arts and Crafts

Yan, inkstone, is used for grinding ink-stick. While writing, dip brush pen into the ink inside the ink-stone. Therefore brush pen, ink, paper and inkstone are collectively known as the "Four Treasures of the Study". There are "four famous ink-stones" in China, namely Duan Inkstone, She Inkstone, Tao Inkstone and Hongsi Inkstone. Among them Duan Inkstone is the most famous and produced in Zhaoqing City, Guangdong Province.

Duan Inkstone has been considered very precious since ancient times. The reasons are as follows: firstly, it is very rare and difficult to find. The raw stone of the Duan Inkstone is under water so mining is not easy. At present, almost all known Duan stone tunnels are depleted and no longer suitable to mine. Secondly, Duan Inkstone raw stones are hard, smooth and delicate, so ink grinded by using Duan Inkstone does not stagnate and stays smooth and it does not damage brush pens and helps in writing with ease and the ink endures time longer. Thirdly, Duan Inkstone seems to have "eyes". The eyes are patterns on the stone, some of which are known as "parrot eye" or "hill myna eye",etc. It is extra fun when grinding and writing as the eyes seem to be watching. Fourthly, the technique of making Duan Inkstone is very complicated. The main steps include selecting stone, processing, engraving, polishing and matching box, etc.

Duan Inkstone has high artistic appreciation and collection values, and it was used as one of the imperial tributes in old times. Generally, it is believed that white Duan Inkstone is the best, followed by blue while purple being the worst. The largest Duan Inkstone in record is "Nine Dragons in Duan Stream", which is 4.6 metres long, 3.15 meters wide and 0.45 meters thick, with 13.8 tons of weight, and known as "The Best in China". It is now kept in Duanming Inkstone Carving Factory in Zhaoqing City.

佛山木版年画 Foshan Woodblock New Year Pictures

明清时期，中国的木版年画达到巅峰，形成"中国四大木版年画"，即天津杨柳青、苏州桃花坞、山东潍坊、广东佛山木版年画。

佛山木版年画兴起于明朝永乐年间（1403—1424），至今已经有700多年的历史。佛山木版年画包括门画（俗称门神）、年画、神像画，其中门神年画最多。佛山木版年画吸收佛山剪纸、金漆木雕、染色纸等民间艺术技法，在色彩上，大面积使用红、绿、黄、黑等大色块，画面鲜艳华丽，增添喜庆的气氛，日晒雨淋也不会变色。因此，佛山木版年画有"万年红"的美誉。在表现手法上，善于结合当地的民俗人情，题材选择、线条处理、着色技巧、造型风格都具有广府文化的细腻特征。人物的盔甲、袍带、衣饰上绘有金银纹饰，画面更加丰富、有装饰性，有浓厚的民间画风味，为其他民间年画所罕见。佛山木版年画大多表现神像、历史人物、神话传说、戏曲故事等。

佛山木版年画是中国华南地区著名的民间年画，是广东民俗文化的一朵奇葩，在东南亚及世界各国华人聚居地都有很大的影响。

9 广东工艺美术
Guangdong Arts and Crafts

Chinese Woodblock New Year Picture reached its peak during the Ming and Qing Dynasties. The four major styles of Chinese Woodblock New Year Pictures are from Yangliuqing in Tianjin, Taohuawu in Suzhou, Weifang in Shandong and Foshan in Guangdong.

Foshan Woodblock New Year Pictures emerged from Yongle Years (1403-1424) during the Ming Dynasty and has more than 700 years of history. Foshan Woodblock New Year Pictures include "Door Pictures" (known as Door Gods), New Year Pictures and Pictures of Gods. Most of them are Door God Pictures. Foshan Woodblock New Year Pictures are colourful and gorgeous with a merry and festive atmosphere. They are derived from a lot of folk art techniques such as paper-cut, gilded wood carvings, and dyed paper and mainly use colours of red, green, yellow, and black. However, their colours would not fade for years, even being exposed to the sun and rain. Therefore, Foshan Woodblock New Year Pictures have also got a good reputation known as "Ten Thousand Year Red". As for the technique of expressions, they are fully considered with local custom and have fine and exquisite characteristics of Cantonese culture in many aspects, including selecting themes, using lines, applying colours, shaping, and styling. The custom of using figures, armours, robe belts, and clothing were decorated with gold and silver patterns which made the pictures very decorative and rich in folk art, a style rarely seen in other types of folk New Year Pictures. The most common themes of Foshan Woodblock New Year Pictures were God statues, historical figures, myths or legends, opera, and play themes.

Foshan Woodblock New Year Pictures are famous Chinese folk paintings in southern China and are considered a wonder of Guangdong's folk culture. They are very popular among Chinese communities around the world, especially in Southeast Asia.

广彩 Cantonese Porcelain

广彩是广州地区釉上彩瓷艺术的简称，指广州烧制的织金彩瓷及其采用的低温釉上彩装饰技法，又叫"广东彩""广州织金彩瓷"。广彩主要用以外销。

广彩始于明代，当时的广州工匠借用西方的"金胎烧珐琅"技法，采用进口材料，创制出"铜胎烧珐琅"技法，后来把这种方法用在白瓷胎上，成为著名的珐琅彩，这是广州彩瓷的萌芽，初期只使用三种颜色。到清朝发展到五种颜色，清朝乾隆年间逐步形成独特的艺术风格，至今已经有300多年的历史。

广东商人从景德镇运来瓷坯，采用江西粉彩[①]技艺仿照西洋彩画的方法加以彩绘，再进行焙烧。后来，广彩继承明代彩瓷的艺术特色，吸收西洋画法，绘上具有广东地方特色的图案，逐渐形成独特的艺术风格，并将许多图案固定下来，成为广彩的传统花款，如花篮、龙凤、彩蝶、金鱼、古代人物等。最常用的构图方法是用花边图案围出几个形状各异的空格，在空格内绘上花草、景物、人物。有的不画圈格，而进行满花彩绘，表现一花多姿、百花齐放的景象。

广彩的风格特点有：运用中国织锦图案的手法，构图严谨、绘工精细；利用各种颜色和金银水进行钩、描、织、填，光彩夺目、富丽堂皇；构图设计讲究完整、统一、和谐。

---

①粉彩是在瓷胎上彩绘、经低温烧成的彩绘方法。

9 广东工艺美术
Guangdong Arts and Crafts

Cantonese porcelain is the short name for Cantonese colour porcelain art. It specifically refers to the art form of glazing colour onto porcelain in a style that was created in the Canton region by using low temperature glazing techniques of colouring and decorating, also known as Cantonese glazing porcelain. Cantonese porcelains are mainly sold abroad.

Cantonese porcelain began during the Ming Dynasty, and Cantonese artisans learned the Western techniques of "Gold Enamel" and then created "Copper Enamel" techniques on imported materials. Later they adopted these techniques on white porcelain bodies, which are now well-known as glazed porcelain. Original forms of Cantonese porcelain only used three colours, but during the Qing Dynasty the number of colours used increased to five, and then gradually developed unique styles during the Qianlong Years. It dates back to more than 300 years ago.

In the beginning, Cantonese potters brought in porcelain bases from Jingdezhen and painted them using Jiangxi pastel painting [①] techniques but mimicking Western paintings before firing in kilns. Later on, Cantonese porcelain inherited the art styles of the Ming Dynasty ceramics, influenced by Western painting techniques and used pictures and patterns with Guangdong local features, which gradually formed a unique artistic style. A number of patterns have become classic and traditional models, such as flower baskets, dragon and phoenix, butterflies, goldfish, historical figures, etc. The most common design was to make a number of spaces with different shapes by using outlined lace patterns, then paint flowers, landscape sceneries and figures within the spaces. Some paintings had no such kind of spaces but were painted with images showing full flowers flourishing.

The features of Cantonese porcelain include: using Chinese brocade pattern with rigorous composition and fine and exquisite painted works; using a variety of colours including gold and silver inks for drafting, sketching, drawing, and filling, which become dazzling and magnificent; paying high attention to integrity, unity, and harmony of the design.

---

① Pastel painting is a technique of painting colours on porcelain bases, then firing in a kiln with a relatively low temperature.

广东文化与社会 Cantonese Culture and Society

广式家具 Cantonese Furniture

广式家具一般指在广东省生产的、具有广东特色的家具。明末清初,很多西方传教士来到中国,加强了东西方文化的交流。作为中国对外贸易和文化交流重要门户的广州,清朝中期的时候,商业建筑大都已经开始模仿西方的形式,如骑楼。与建筑相适应的家具也逐渐形成了新的款式。用料粗大、体质厚重、雕刻繁复的广式家具开始流行,并对中国传统的家具式样和风格产生巨大的冲击,如束腰、家具腿足重雕刻,装饰采用当时流行的"西番莲"花纹。一直以来都是典型"清式"的广式家具在此时形成了自己的风格。

广式家具的特点有:①用料统一且粗大。广式家具一般采用清一色的同一木质,如紫檀、酸枝,决不掺杂其他木材。不论弯曲度有多大,广式家具的腿足、立柱等主要构件一般都不拼接,而是用一整块木料制成。②装饰花纹雕刻深厚,磨工精细。广式家具的雕刻风格受到西方建筑雕刻的很大影响,雕刻花纹隆起较高,个别部位甚至近似圆雕。花纹表面滑润如玉,丝毫不留刀砍斧凿的痕迹。③装饰花纹以西方的"西番莲"居多。通常以一朵或几朵花为中心,向四周延伸,而且上下左右对称。如果装饰在圆形器物上,花朵的枝叶大多是循环的形状,各面纹饰巧妙衔接,首尾相连,自成一体。

广州市每年都举行国际家具博览会,如今已经举办了38届,在世界范围内有很大的影响。

9 广东工艺美术
Guangdong Arts and Crafts

Cantonese furniture refers to that made in Guangdong and with Cantonese features. From the late Ming Dynasty to the early Qing Dynasty there were many priests who came to China from Western countries and enhanced culture exchange between China and the West. Guangzhou, as one of the most important gates to foreign trade and culture exchange, started to adopt Western business architectures during the mid-Qing Dynasty, such as Qilou (Riding Building). As a result, furniture of new style was introduced to fit with the buildings. Furniture with big wood blocks, heavy weights and detailed carvings became more popular and had great influences on traditional Chinese furniture designs and styles, such as girdles and carvings on furniture feet and Xi Fanlian (Western Lotus) patterns. Cantonese furniture started to form its style during the same periods, whereas it had been the typical Qing style furniture.

Cantonese furniture has a number features: Firstly, it uses uniform and big sized materials. Cantonese furniture normally uses the same type wood material for a single piece of furniture, such as, red sandalwood and rosewood, and not mixed with other types of timbers. When making a piece of furniture, the main components like feet and vertical columns, regardless of how much curvature, are made from one single timber, not from jointed pieces. Secondly, it has deep carved and finely ground decorative patterns. The carving style on Cantonese furniture is greatly influenced by the Western architectures and sculptures, and curving patterns are uplifted high and some are even close to a circular sculpture. The surfaces of carving pattern are as smooth as jade and do not leave any traces of chisel or knife work. The third feature is the popular lotus pattern. This pattern usually starts with one or several flowers as the centre, extending to all directions and is symmetrical in the upper and lower, left and right sides. If on a circular piece, the flower branches and leaves are in circular shape, the patterns are elaborately connected each other, end to end, becoming a whole piece.

The International Furniture Fair is held in Guangzhou City annually. So far it has had 38 sessions, and is well-known worldwide.

广绣 Cantonese Embroidery

刺绣指使用针线在织物上绣制各种装饰图案及其产品,在中国已经有 3000 多年的历史。中国刺绣主要有江苏的苏绣、湖南的湘绣、四川的蜀绣和广东的粤绣。粤绣又叫广绣,指广府地区的刺绣工艺品。

广绣使用丝绒、真丝、金线、银线、金绒混合等材料。其中金银绣具有很强的装饰性,构图饱满匀称,色彩辉煌,富丽华贵。

广绣有盘金刺绣和丝绒刺绣两个种类。盘金刺绣以金线为主,辅以彩纷刺绣,金碧辉煌、灿烂夺目。丝绒刺绣开丝纤细,色彩缤纷,绣出的花鸟尤其精美。

广绣的色彩主要有威彩和淡彩两类。威彩以较饱满的色彩为主调,淡彩以三间色为主调。色彩根据刺绣品种来确定,比如绣喜帐用威彩,绣文房用品用淡彩。

Embroidery refers to embroidered fabric products using needle and thread with a variety of decorative patterns, and it has had over 3,000 years of history in China. The main Chinese embroideries are Suzhou Embroidery, Hunan Embroidery, Sichuan Embroidery, and Yue Embroidery. Yue Embroidery is also known as Cantonese Embroidery, which is a well-known embroidery art product from the Guangdong region.

Cantonese Embroidery uses silk-velvet, silk, gold and silver threads, as well as golden couching. Among them, embroidery products with gold and silver threads are beautifully decorative, and the pictures are normally well-balanced with magnificent colours and richness.

There are two main types of Cantonese Embroidery, namely Gold Thread Embroidery and Silk-Velvet Embroidery. The Gold Thread Embroidery mainly uses gold thread but is also supplemented by other colour embroideries, so it is splendid and dazzling. The Silk-Velvet Embroidery uses very thin threads and is normally colourful, in particular with beautiful flowers and birds designs.

Cantonese Embroidery mainly uses two classes of colour, rich and light. Rich colour uses all sorts of colours, but the light colour uses only three colours (orange, purple and green) in alternating ways. Depending on the product needs, the colour can be different, for example, wedding curtains use rich colour, while study stationeries usually use light colour.

广绣的特色产品有人物绣和花鸟绣,其中人物绣是广绣的主要产品之一。根据画稿的不同要求,以虚实、施疏、层层叠绣、渗绣、线面结合等绣制方法,使人物形神兼备、栩栩如生。花鸟绣善于体现平、齐、细、密、均、光、和、顺的艺术风格,构图精密、色彩秀丽、针法多变。

从清朝起,广绣就闻名海内外,在世界上享有很高的声誉。清朝中期,许多外国商人慕名来到广州订货,有的还专门带来外国国王的肖像、耶稣像或者图画照片进行来样加工。北京故宫博物院收藏有很多优秀的广绣作品。

The specialities of Cantonese Embroidery include figure embroidery, flower and bird embroidery. The figure embroidery is one of the main products. According to the different requirements of drawings of the actual situation, different techniques will be applied, such as solid and empty, sparse and dense, overlaying, penetrating, linear and surfaces, with the figures vivid and lifelike. Flower and bird embroideries are good at expressing artistic style of smooth, tidy, fine, dense, uniform, light, soft and fluent with precise composition, beautiful colour and sophisticated needle work.

From the Qing Dynasty, the Cantonese Embroidery became well-known at home and abroad. During the mid-Qing Dynasty, many foreign businessmen came to Guangzhou to place orders, and some specially brought portraits of foreign kings and Jesus, and photographs or drawings for custom products. There are many excellent collections of Cantonese Embroidery art works in the Beijing Palace Museum.

广州盆景 Cantonese Bonsai

盆景是以植物或山石为基本材料,在盆内表现自然景观的园林艺术。盆景起源于中国。中国盆景艺术有五个流派:苏州、扬州、四川、安徽、岭南。广州盆景属于岭南盆景,明清时期开始产生,1949年以后形成独特的风格。

广州人非常喜爱盆景,很多家庭都会把盆景摆放在天台、阳台、客厅、书房、走道,用来美化环境、陶冶性情。

广州盆景包括树桩盆景和石山盆景。栽种树桩盆景的主要方法是选择树形、布局构图、挑选良干、梳理根系、修整枝条、精心培植。树桩盆景一般用月橘、榕树、水松、龙柏、榆树、满天星、黄杨、罗汉松、山桔、相思树等树种。石山盆景一般用英石、方解石、珊瑚石、砂积石等石料。

广州盆景的特点有:①师法自然,突出枝干技巧,追求自然美与人工美的结合,所以广州盆景被誉为"活的中国画";②注重景与盆的造型搭配,追求景与盆的和谐协调;③善于修剪,不露刀剪痕迹。这是广州盆景最大的特点。

广州盆景深受港澳同胞以及欧美、东南亚等地华人的喜爱。广州市芳村是广东省最早、最著名的"盆景之乡"。建于1956年的西苑公园以栽种、陈列盆景为主题,位于广州市流花湖畔,面积5000平方米,是海内外闻名的"岭南盆景之家"。

9 广东工艺美术
Guangdong Arts and Crafts

Bonsai art uses plants and rocks as basic materials and concentrates the natural beauty of gardens inside a small pot or basin. Bonsai was originated from China. There are five schools of Chinese bonsai art, namely Suzhou, Yangzhou, Sichuan, Anhui and Lingnan. Guangzhou Bonsai is part of the Lingnan School and started during the Ming and Qing Dynasties, and then established its own unique style after 1949.

Cantonese love bonsais. Many families like to place bonsais on rooftops or balconies, in living rooms, study rooms or hallways to create beautiful and pleasant environments.

Cantonese bonsai has two main classes, tree stump and rock formations. The main techniques of making a tree stump bonsai include the shape selection of the tree stump, overall layout design, root trimming, tree wiring, caring and maintenance. Normally, tree stump bonsais use orange, banyan, yew, cypress, elm, baby's breath, boxwood, podocarpus, mountains orange, acacia plants and foliage as well as others. While rock formation bonsais use rock materials like cristobalite, calcite, coral, and sand rocks.

Cantonese bonsai has three main features: the first is focusing on harmony of nature and uses of tree branches, pursuing combinations of natural and artificial beauties, therefore Guangzhou bonsai is known as "Live Chinese Painting"; the second is paring of the pot and the model, focusing on harmony between the scenery and the selected pot; the third is trimming technique, and there is no trace of cutting and trimming revealed.

Guangzhou bonsais are very popular among the compatriots in Hong Kong and Macao, and overseas Chinese in Southeast Asia, Europe and America. Fang Village in Guangzhou is the earliest and well-known "Hometown of Bonsai". Xiyuan Park, which was built in 1956 and is situated by the Liuhua Lake in Guangzhou, mainly grows and displays bonsais. It has an area of 5,000 square metres and enjoys a well earned reputation of "Home of Lingnan Bonsai" at home and abroad.

雷州石狗 Leizhou Stone Dog Sculptures

广东省的雷州人认为,狗最有灵性,能够祛邪消灾、赐财生福、添丁延寿。当地的先民甚至崇拜灵犬,给小孩取名也带有"狗"字,如"狗仔""狗生""昵狗"等。雷州境内现存的古石狗大概有2万只,年代较早的石狗是南北朝时期古雷州州治旧址附近"石狗坡"的石狗,距今有1400多年。

雷州石狗一般用玄武岩雕刻而成,最大的石狗连座高1.3米,重约800公斤;小的高10厘米,重约0.5公斤;一般的石狗跟真狗差不多大。雷州石狗的总体艺术风格是写意的。从造型上,可以分为三个时期:早期,即春秋至秦汉时期,造型粗犷质朴,形态简洁,昂首向天,神情肃穆,具有天人相通的图腾特征;中期,即隋唐至宋元时期,注重结构、线条的表现,突出生殖器,反映祈求多子的淳朴民风;晚期,即明清时期,大多使用拟人的手法,有人面狗身的造型,形神兼备,雕刻精美,纹饰细腻。

2002年,中国第一家石狗博物馆在广东省雷州市雷城镇二元塔公园建成,石狗博物馆收集有1000多只大小不等、形态各异的石狗,堪称"南方兵马俑"。

9 广东工艺美术
Guangdong Arts and Crafts

Leizhou people in Guangdong Province think that dogs are the most intelligent animals and can help them to avoid bad luck and disasters, bring in good fortunes and wealth, live longer lives, and have more offsprings. Leizhou people even worship dogs and use the word "Gou"(dog) for names of children such as "Gou Zai" (little dog), "Gou Sheng" (dog born), and "Ni Gou" (dear dog). There are about twenty thousand ancient dog stone sculptures in Leizhou area, of which the earliest can date back to the Southern and Northern Dynasties about 1,400 years ago.

Leizhou dog stone sculptures are normally made of basalt, with the largest measuring 1.3 meters high, including the base, and weighing about 800 kilograms. A smaller one is only 10 centimetres in height and weighs about 0.5 kilograms. The mostly common stone dogs are about the size of real dogs. The style of the Leizhou dog stone sculptures is impressionistic. There are roughly three historic periods: The first starts in the early part of the Spring and Autumn Dynasties going through the Qin Dynasty and ending at some point in the Han Dynasty where the shapes of the sculptures were primitive and simple. The heads of the dogs were pointed up as if looking at the sky with a solemn faces, similar to totemic pictures which means being connected with the Heaven. The second period, spans from the Sui and Tang Dynasties to the Song and Yuan Dynasties and focuses on shapes and lines, highlighting the genitalia, and reflecting the wish of the Leizhou people to have more children. The last period, stretches from the late Ming and Qing Dynasties, and mimics humans and some sculptures have a dog body with a human face, with vivid and beautiful carvings and exquisite decorations.

The very first museum of stone dog sculptures was opened in Sanyuan Tower Park, Leicheng Town, Leizhou City, Guangdong Province, in 2002. The museum has collected more than 1,000 different stone dogs with various sizes and shapes. The museum is also referred to as "Southern Terracotta Warriors and Horses".

木雕 Wood-carvings

木雕是雕塑的一种。广东省的潮州木雕主要用来装饰建筑、神器、家具、案头等。因为潮州木雕往往会贴上纯金箔,显得金碧辉煌,所以又称潮州金漆木雕。潮州木雕与东阳木雕并列为中国民间两大木雕体系。

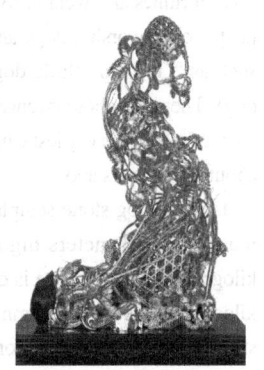

潮州木雕选用当地出产的普通木材。建筑装饰用的木雕一般采用比较粗大的杉木。家具器物类的木雕大多采用樟木,因为樟木的质地并不坚密,但有一定的韧性,而且容易雕刻,雕刻之后,贴上金箔,显得辉煌灿烂,而且能够抗潮防蛀,不至于变形、崩裂或者腐朽。

潮州木雕有全贴金的金漆木雕、五彩描金的彩雕、清一色髹红(或黑)的漆雕、保持原木纹理的素雕等,其中金漆木雕最为有名。不少木雕贴有金箔进行装饰,以黑漆或者五彩加以烘托,前者称为"黑色装金",后者称为"五彩装金"。

潮州木雕的品种很多,包括花鸟虫鱼、四季果品、江海水族、珍禽瑞兽、神话传说、古代戏曲等,大致可以分为图案、禽兽、山水、博古、花果草虫、仙佛人物。

潮州木雕工艺精湛、玲珑剔透、金碧辉煌,深受东南亚地区华侨的喜爱,在世界上也享有很高的声誉。

9 广东工艺美术
Guangdong Arts and Crafts

Wood-carving is one type of sculpture. Wood-carvings in the Chaozhou area of Guangdong Province are mainly used for decorations related to architecture, temple artifacts, furniture. Chaozhou wood-carvings are normally enwrapped with pure gold leaf, looking golden and shiny; therefore it is also known as gold lacquer wood-carvings. Alongside with Dongyang wood-carvings, Chaozhou wood-carvings are one of two main Chinese folk wood-carving styles.

Chaozhou wood-carving uses ordinary wood from local trees. Large-sized logs are usually used for the wood-carvings of architecture decorations, but for furniture wood-carvings, camphor is normally used. Camphor is not very hard and dense, however quite tough, which makes it easy for carving. After a sculpture is finished, it is pasted with gold leaf, and the wood-carving displays a magnificently golden sheen, which is also damp and moth resistant and will not easily become deformed, cracked, or rotten.

There are many types of Chaozhou wood-carvings, including gold leaf, five-colour gilded with gold, pure red or black lacquer, carvings with the original wood pattern, with gold leaf wood-carvings being the most famous among them all. Many wood-carvings use black or five-coloured backgrounds decorated with gold leafs, of which the former one is called "Gold with Black" and the latter "Gold with Five-colours".

There are many kinds of themes of Chaozhou wood-carvings, including flowers, birds, fish, insects, seasonal fruits, creatures from the rivers and seas, rare birds and auspicious animals, figures of myths and legends from traditional operas and drama, etc. They can also be classified as animals, landscapes, flowers, fruits, vegetables and figures of gods or Buddha.

Due to their exquisite quality and magnificent display, Chaozhou wood-carvings are very popular among overseas Chinese in Southeast Asia, and they also have a good reputation all over the world.

瓶内画 Inner Painting

瓶内画是用特制的小笔从细小的瓶口进入瓶内,用反手画法,在透明的瓶子内壁上绘出花草、人物、鸟兽、书法等的绘画艺术。

明末清初,西方的鼻烟瓶传入中国,中国人对之进行艺术加工,并不断创新,逐渐形成瓶内画。瓶内画是融汇了中西方文化的一门中国民间艺术,被认为是最具有中国特色的手工艺品之一。瓶内画开始于清朝咸丰年间(1851—1861年),至今已有100多年的历史,形成了北京、山东、河北、广东四大流派。

9 广东工艺美术
Guangdong Arts and Crafts

Inner painting is one kind of painting art on inner walls of transparent bottles. The bottles are painted on the inner walls with flowers, people, animals, and calligraphy using specialized long small brush pens through the narrow bottle neck and a backhand technique.

During the Ming and Qing Dynasties, Western snuff bottles were introduced into China and the Chinese developed it further artistically with innovations, thus inner painting was gradually created. Inner painting is a blend of Western painting techniques and Chinese folk art and culture and is recognized as one of the most special Chinese characteristics in handicrafts. Inner painting began in the Xianfeng Years (1851-1861), during the Qing Dynasty and has had over 100 years of history. There are four main schools of this art, namely Beijing, Shandong, Hebei and Guangdong inner painting.

广东瓶内画只有30多年的历史,以汕头瓶内画为代表。首先用磨砂石将瓶子的内壁打磨成乳白色,使得画面更加清晰,然后开始作画。使用铅丝制成弯钩形的画笔,在笔尖上镶上柔软且富有弹性的狼毫描笔,使执笔方法更加接近普通平面作画。汕头瓶内画受岭南画派的影响,线条纤秀,色彩艳丽,瓶外描金加珐琅彩,金碧辉煌、绚丽多彩。瓶内画的瓶子采用水晶、玻璃、玛瑙等材料,也很美观。瓶体造型有圆形、扁形、椭圆形、连体等,具有较高的欣赏价值和收藏价值。

汕头瓶内画的创始人是吴松龄。汕头瓶内画的绘画工具、绘画技法、构图形式、瓶体造型、瓶外装饰、艺术效果等都自成特色,与北方的瓶内画有很大差异。鼎盛时期是20世纪80年代。遗憾的是,汕头瓶内画出现了后继乏人的状况。

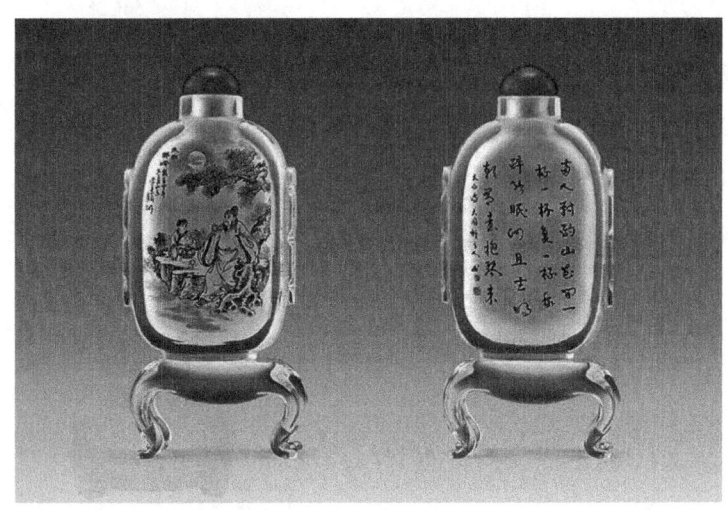

9 广东工艺美术
Guangdong Arts and Crafts

Guangdong inner painting has only 30 years of history, and the majority is Shantou inner painting. To prepare the bottle one must first polish the inner walls to a white surface with a matte polished stone. In this way, the picture will be clearer and then painting can begin. The pen is made from a hook-shaped wire fit on the tip with a soft and flexible Langhao (wolf hair) brush pen, in this way the painter can hold the pen and draw pictures similar to normal painting. Influenced by the Lingnan School of painting, Shantou inner painting has a unique style with elegant lines, gorgeous colors and sometimes with gilded enamel on the outer bottle surface which gives magnificent and splendid effects. The bottles can be crystal, glass, agate, or other like materials which make them all look beautiful. The bottle shapes can be round, flat, oval, siamese, etc. Shantou inner paintings are beautiful in appreciation and valuable as collections.

The founder of Shantou inner painting is Wu Songling. The tools, painting techniques, compositions, forms, shape of the bottles, design and artistic effects are unique. They are distinctively different from other schools, in particular Northern schools. The heyday of Shantou inner painting was during the 1980's. Unfortunately, there is lack of successors continuing Shantou inner painting.

吴川泥塑 Wuchuan Clay Sculptures

泥塑是以泥土为原料、用手捏制成各种形象的一种民间手工艺,俗称"彩塑""泥玩"。新石器时期,中国就已经有了泥塑。

吴川泥塑,又称"泥公仔"。唐朝时,广东佛山廖岭居民迁移到吴川梅菉镇瓦窑村,把佛山精湛的陶瓷工艺带到吴川。

泥塑用稻草或竹木作支架,泥土作材料,现场制作,泥塑和真人一样大,具有展出空间大、写实性和娱乐性的特点,是没有功利性的节庆民俗活动。泥塑题材有历史故事、神话故事、民间传说。如今,出现了水上彩塑和活动彩塑,具有浓厚的乡土气息和时代特色,配上灯光、音响、舞美设计,集电、光、声、动于一体,显得更加流光溢彩、美不胜收。

传说在明朝洪武年间,皇帝派遣官吏四处选美,民间对此怨声载道。于是,梅菉头村群众趁闹元宵的机会,特意捏造了一套丑化皇帝和皇后的泥塑,眼大、肚大、脚大、乳大、耳大,形象非常丑陋。官员很生气,制作泥塑的作者解释说:"皇上眼大看得准,肚大有福分,脚大稳乾坤,乳大养子民,耳大听民言,这有何不好?"官员无话可说。官员走后,群众干脆把泥塑推倒,称为送"泥鬼"。以后便成为习俗,每年元宵造一次"泥鬼",就要送一次"泥鬼"。

9 广东工艺美术
Guangdong Arts and Crafts

Clay sculpture is a type of hand-made folk crafts using clay as the raw material. It is also widely known as "colour sculpture" or "clay figures". The earliest clay sculptures found in China can date back to the Neolithic Period.

Wuchuan clay sculpture is also called "clay figures". During the Tang Dynasty, some migrants went to Wayao Village, Wuchuan from Foshan Liaoling area in Guangdong, and they brought superb Foshan ceramic technology to Wuchuan.

When making a clay sculpture, straw, bamboo or wood could be used as "the bones" (frames), then clay as raw material for the body. It could be a life-like production with the same size of a real person. The sculptures are lively, vivid and entertaining and especially suitable for folk festival activities. The popular themes of clay sculptures are historical stories, myths and folklores. Nowadays, people have also created floating colour sculptures and acting colour sculptures with a rich, local flavour and characteristics of the times. They are even more colourful and beautiful together with lighting, music and stage effects.

According to a legend, Hongwu, the emperor of the Ming Dynasty sent special envoys all over the country selecting beautiful girls so people suffered and had a lot of complaints. Therefore, people in Meilutou Village took an opportunity during the Lantern Festival to make some clay sculptures of the emperor and empress in ugly ways. They had big eyes, big bellies, big feet, big breasts and big ears. The envoy officials became furious but the clay makers explained cleverly, "The big eyes mean they see things rightly; a big belly means great fortune; big feet symbolize stable emperor power; big breasts mean to feed people and big ears mean to listen to people's voice. What is wrong?" The envoy officials became speechless and left. People later on even pushed the clay sculptures down on the ground and called it sending away "clay ghosts". Since then it became a tradition that people make "clay ghosts" and then send the "clay ghosts" away in the Lantern Festival.

阳江风筝 Yangjiang Kites

风筝起源于中国的春秋时期,至今已经有2000多年的历史。南北朝时期,风筝开始用于军事,成为传递信息的工具。隋唐时期,造纸业发达,民间开始用纸来裱糊风筝。宋朝,放风筝成为人们喜爱的户外活动。风筝的形状主要模仿大自然的生物,如鸟、兽、虫、鱼,也模仿神话传说中的人物。中国风筝形成了"五大流派"。如今,有"南有阳江,北有潍坊"的说法。

9 广东工艺美术
Guangdong Arts and Crafts

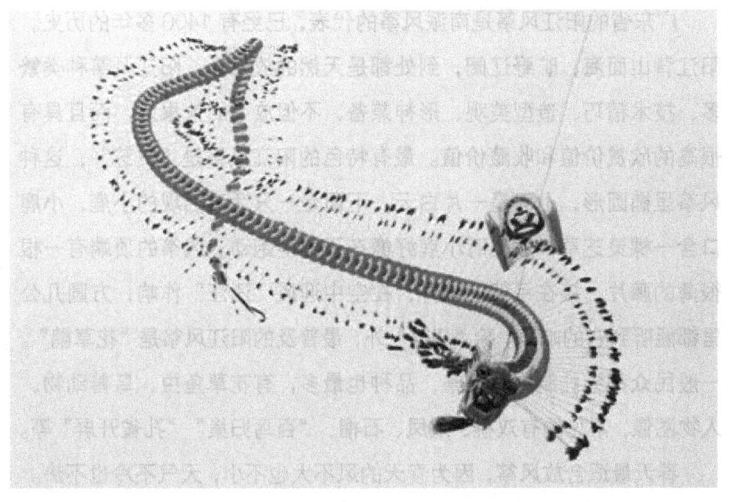

Kites originated from the Spring and Autumn period in China and have had more than 2,000 years of history. During the Northern and Southern Dynasties, kites began to be used by the army as a means of passing messages. During the Sui and Tang Dynasties, with the developed paper manufacturing industry, people began to make paper kites. In the Song Dynasty, flying kites became one of the favorite outdoor activities. Kites normally took the shapes of insects, fish, birds and animals, as well as the figures from myths and legends. There are "five schools" of Chinese kites and there is a well-known saying, "Southern Yangjiang and Northern Weifang".

广东省的阳江风筝是南派风筝的代表,已经有1400多年的历史。阳江背山面海,旷野辽阔,到处都是天然的放飞场。阳江风筝种类繁多、技术精巧、造型美观、形神兼备,不但放飞的效果好,而且具有很高的欣赏价值和收藏价值。最有特色的阳江风筝是"灵芝",这种风筝呈椭圆形,上面是一片白云,下面是一只活灵活现的小鹿,小鹿口含一棵灵芝草,放飞时小鹿好像在不停地跑动。风筝的顶端有一根很薄的藤片,接在弓架上张开,在空中迎风"汪汪"作响,方圆几公里都能听到它的响声。除"灵芝"外,最普及的阳江风筝是"花草鹞"。一般民众都会扎制这种风筝,品种也最多,有花草鱼虫、鸟兽动物、人物图像,常见的有双桃、双凤、石榴、"百鸟归巢""孔雀开屏"等。

春天最适合放风筝,因为春天的风不大也不小,天气不冷也不热。春季草长莺飞,花红柳绿。放飞时,远望蓝天,大脑高度集中,好像人和自然在对话,能使人心情开朗、身心愉悦。

1991年,阳江市建成南国风筝竞技场,总面积12万平方米,可同时容纳30万人放风筝,是中国最大的风筝放飞场。1993年,阳江市被评为"中国风筝之乡",阳江市因此被称为"纸鹞城"。

9 广东工艺美术
Guangdong Arts and Crafts

Yangjiang kites in Guangdong are the representative of the Southern school and has over 1,400 years of history. Yangjiang area rests on a mountain and faces sea, with vast fields especially suitable for kite-flying. There are a variety of kites which were all made with sophisticated skills, beautiful and elegant in appearance. They not only could fly well, but are also valuable for appreciation and collecting. The most distinctive Yangjiang kites are "Lingzhi" (Ganoderma lucidum), which is typically an oval shape. The upper part has a white cloud and the lower part a vivid deer which holds a Lingzhi in its mouth and looks like it is running while the kite is flying. There is a thin bamboo slice at the top of kite which makes a "barking" sound in air that can be heard several kilometers in radius. In addition, "Lingzhi", the most popular of Yangjiang kites are "Paper Harrier". Almost anyone can make this type of kite and the most popular themes include flowers, fishes, insects, birds, animals and human figures, with the most commonly seen varieties being twin-peaches, twin-phoenix, pomegranates, "birds flying home", "speacocks spreading their tails", etc.

The best time for flying kites is spring because the wind is moderate and the weather is mild. In spring, grasses are growing and birds are flying, and there are red flowers and green trees everywhere. It is very pleasant and cheerful for anyone to fly a kite in the blue sky.

In 1991, "South China Kite Arena" was built in Yangjiang with a total area of 120,000 square meters, and it is the largest kite flying site in China accommodating 300,000 people flying kites at the same time. In 1993, Yangjiang was named "Hometown of the Chinese Kites" and is also known as the "Hometown of Paper Harrier".

10 广东民俗

Guangdong Folk Traditions

"意头" "Yi Tou"

"意头"就是吉利、好运的意思。广东人很讲究"意头",什么事都要图吉利,例如菜名、数字、习俗等。

"意头"大多采用谐音的方式把事物和吉祥的意思联系起来。比如春节时的鱼象征年年有余,

葱、蒜代表聪明、精打细算,芹菜寓意勤力,发菜、生菜谐音发财、生财,炸虾球就是生意兴隆,发菜蚝豉谐音发财好市,生菜猪手谐音生财就收。酒店的很多菜肴也蕴含"意头",比如百年鸿运、花开富贵、点点心意、锦绣虾、喜洋洋、花好月圆等。

广东人喜欢的数字有6、8、9。6谐音"陆",表示顺利;8谐音"发",表示发财;9谐音"久",表示长久。因此,广东人喜欢选用这些数字作为电话号码和车牌号码等。广东人不喜欢数字4,因为4谐音"死",所以广东人忌讳用4,比如广东的高楼大厦的第4层往往标为3A,第14层标为13A,等等。

逛花市是广东春节的传统习俗。过春节逛花市时,广东人经常会买一些花、柑(谐音"金")、桔(谐音"吉")等回家,寓意新的一年花开富贵、大吉大利。

10 广东民俗
Guangdong Folk Traditions

"Yi Tou" means good fortunes or good luck. Cantonese are very careful or even fussy about "Yi Tou", and everything is centered around being lucky, such as names of dishes, numbers or festival customs.

Generally, "Yi Tou" takes the sound or meaning of things and links it with good fortune. For example, the character for fish (pronounce as Yu) in the Spring Festival symbolises "having more (Yu) year after year", whereas onion and garlic sound like intelligence or careful planning in Chinese; celery means hard working; Fa Cai (a kind of weed like plant found in desert) indicates getting wealthier; and lettuce would be for more fortune. Restaurant dishes like deep-fried shrimp balls mean business is booming; oysters with Fa Cai mean more fortune and good business; pork paws with lettuce sounds like collecting money, etc. In hotels one can see more dishes with "Yi Tou", such as "Bai Nian Hong Yun (Hundred Years of Fortune)", "Hua Kai Fu Gui (Wealth Blossoming)", "Dian Dian Xin Yi (Little Treats)", "Jin Xiu Xia (Magnificent Prawns)", "Xi Yang Yang (Happiness)", "Hua Hao Yue Yuan (Beautiful Flowers and Full Moon)", just to name a few.

Cantonese like the numbers six, eight, and nine. Six sounds like "Lu", meaning to go on smoothy; eight is for "fa", meaning to get richer; and nine sounds like "jiu", meaning long time. Therefore, they like to use these numbers for telephone numbers or vehicle registration numbers. They dislike the number four because it sounds like "dead", so four becomes a taboo number. For example, buildings in Guangdong often have floor 3A, instead of 4, or 13A rather than 14.

It is a custom for the Cantonese to visit the flower markets during Chinese New Year days. They will normally buy symbolic coloured or significant flowers and plants, orange (sounding like "gold") or citrus (sounding like "fortune"), for bringing homes good lucks in the New Year.

工夫茶 Kungfu Tea

工夫茶,也叫功夫茶,不是一种茶叶或茶类的名称,而是一种泡茶的方法。沏泡、品饮工夫茶的方式都非常讲究。

喝茶能解暑、减肥、消除疲劳。清晨或者吃鱼腥之后用茶叶水漱口,能有效去除腥臭味。现代医学科学发现,喝茶,尤其是喝乌龙茶和绿茶,可以防癌。

泡工夫茶的过程是:泡茶时,放七成茶叶就够。放茶叶时,要把粗叶放在茶壶底部和滴嘴处,将细叶放在中层,再将粗叶放在上面,这样茶味可以逐渐散发,出茶就会均匀。然后用开水冲茶,冲茶时要沿壶边冲入,使开水有力地冲击茶叶,使茶的香味快速挥发。冲水一定要满,从壶口轻轻刮去茶沫,盖好盖子,再用开水淋在茶壶上。倒茶之前要用开水淋杯子,淋杯时开水要直冲杯心。最后是倒茶。倒茶时茶壶不要拿得太高,太高的话,容易激起泡沫,茶香味也容易散失,这是对客人的不尊敬。倒茶要快,使香味不散失,保持茶的热度。倒茶时要杯杯轮流洒匀,而且不要让余水留在茶壶中。

喝工夫茶时,一般三人用两个杯,四人用三个杯,五人以上用四个杯。这样,当每一轮茶倒完,总有一个人要轮空。因此,在倒完第一轮茶之后,小辈要敬长辈、主人要让客人。

Kungfu tea is not actually a type of tea, but a particular brewing method. One needs to follow special procedures to make and drink Kungfu tea.

Drinking tea can remove inner heat, help in weight control and ease fatigue. Rinsing mouth with tea in the morning or after eating sea foods can effectively remove the stench. It is proven by modern medical science that drinking tea, especially oolong tea and green tea, can help in preventing cancer.

The procedures of making Kungfu tea are as follows: in a teapot, fill with about 70% tea leaves. The arrangement of putting the leaves into the pot is to place at the bottom the big leaves, then the middle, small and tiny leaves, followed by the big leaves again on the top. In this way the flavour can be gradually extracted and distributed, and the tea will look pure and clear. Then pour boiling water into the tea pot along the edge, so that the strong impact of hot water on the tea leaves will help rapid evaporation of the aroma. The pot must be completely filled. However, there will be some foam or tea residuals floating at the top, which must be gently scraped. Replace the lid; then pour more hot water on the outside of the teapot. Prior to using the tea cups, the cups must be washed using boiling water, so pour the hot water straight into the cups centre. Finally, the last procedure is serving tea. Do not hold the teapot too high while serving the tea, because it will generate bubbles and cause loss of flavour if the teapot is too high, and it also shows disrespect to the guests. The tea needs to be served quickly, so as to keep as much flavour as possible. When serving many cups, make sure every cup gets the same amount of tea but also don't leave any tea in the pot when finished.

While drinking Kungfu tea, normally there are only two cups for three people, three cups for four, four cups for more than five people. In this way, when each round of the drinking tea is finished, there is always at least one person to be in waiting. Thus, after the first round of tea, young people need to pay respect to their elders by serving the tea, and the host needs to serve the guests.

花市 Flower Markets

花市是销售花卉和园艺用品的集市,有长期性和临时性的花市。在唐代,中国就已经出现花市。目前,以成都和广州的花市最有名。

广州的气候适合种花,已经有1000多年的历史,所以,广州又叫"花城"。其中一年一度的迎春花市最引人注目,影响也最大。广州迎春花市在19世纪60年代形成,从每年的农历腊月二十七或二十八开始,一连三天举办。

迎春花市体现了广州的春节习俗,反映了广州人"讲意头"的传统。春节时,广州人喜欢种金桔、插桃花、供水仙。粤语中的"桔"和"吉"同音,金桔象征大吉大利。桃花象征大展宏图,青年人则希望借此走桃花运,买一株桃花摆放在家中,祈求来年找到自己心爱的伴侣。水仙象征富贵吉祥,每年腊月初,广州人会把水仙买回来精心培植,通过水温和日照控制花期,让它在除夕或正月初一时开放,寓意"花开富贵",有个好兆头。花的价格也都和发财致富有关,喜欢用数字"3""8""9",因为与"生""发""久"谐音,寓意生猛、发财、长久。

广州市各个区都有花市,如天河公园花市、越秀西湖花市、荔湾路花市、海珠区滨江西路和宝岗大道花市等。

Flower market is the wholesale and retailer market for flowers and gardening tools, and there are long-term and temporary flower markets. They can date back to the Tang Dynasty. Today, flower markets in Chengdu and Guangzhou are the most well-known.

The climate in the Guangzhou is very suitable for growing flowers, and the flower business has already had over 1,000 years of history; therefore Guangzhou is also called the City of Flowers. One of the most attractive and influential annual events in the city is Ying Chun (Welcome Spring) Flower Market. The Ying Chun Flower Market in Guangzhou started in the 1860's, and it lasts three days from 27th or 28th December (Chinese Lunar Calendar) every year.

The Ying Chun Flower Market is a good example of the Chinese New Year traditions in Guangzhou, and it also reflects the custom "Yi Tou" (wishing good luck). During the Spring Festival period, Cantonese like growing flowers such as kumquats, peaches and daffodil. In Cantonese the word "orange" sounds similar to "good fortune"; kumquat symbolises very good luck; peach is a symbol of great progress in career or business, but young people think of the peach blossom as good luck in love, hoping that with a peach flower at home it could bring a beloved companion in the coming year. Daffodil symbolises wealth and good fortune and at the beginning of December every year, the Cantonese will carefully choose, take home to cultivate the daffodil, and grow it under controlled conditions of humidity, temperatures, and sunlight, with the aim of its blooming on New Years' Eve or New Years' Day, implying "Blossoming of wealth and fortune ", which is a good token. Even the prices of flowers are related to luck, and the most popular numbers are 3, 8 and 9, transliterating as good health, prosperity and longevity.

In Guangzhou City, every district has flower markets, such as Tianhe Park Flower Market, Yuexiu Xihu Flower Market, Liwan Road Flower Market, Haizhu Binjiangxilu and Baogang Road Flower Markets, etc.

广东文化与社会 Cantonese Culture and Society

菊花会 Chrysanthemum Fairs

小榄镇是广东省中山市的一个镇。小榄人喜欢菊花,更喜欢种菊花,因而小榄有"菊城"的美称。小榄人栽培、扎制菊花的工艺代代相传,扎制的立菊特别好看。

小榄每"60年一次大展,10年一次小展"的菊花会以"自然、人文、花海、菊城"为特色,以菊花造景为主,突出栽培技艺,是广东菊文化的一次盛会。改革开放以后,小榄镇每三年举办一届中型的菊花会,每年举办一次菊花欣赏会。菊花会会期从几天到十几天不等,主要包括赏菊、赛菊、吟菊、画菊、尝菊、菊花戏等活动。

小榄菊花会是中国菊文化最集中的体现,参与人数很多,文化内涵深厚,具有较高的历史价值和文化价值。中国人认为,菊花品性高洁。小榄菊花会对陶冶性情、提高文化素养、增进文化交流、构建和谐社会都有重要的促进作用。

Xiaolan Town is a small town in Zhongshan City, Guangdong Province. The local people are fond of chrysanthemums and love to grow different species of chrysanthemums, and thus the town has got the name—Town of Chrysanthemum. The techniques of cultivating and making chrysanthemum art works have been passed down from generation to generation, in particular, creating "Standing Chrysanthemum" which is a type of intricate art work.

In Xiaolan, there is a major flower exhibition every 60 years and a regular flower exhibition every 10 years. The main features of the exhibition include "Great Nature, Local Culture, Flower Sea and Chrysanthemum Town". Most of the art works are chrysanthemum displays, showing off cultivation techniques and they are the major events of the chrysanthemum culture. Since the reform and opening-up, Xiaolan hosts medium-scaled chrysanthemum fairs every three years and a chrysanthemum show once a year. The chrysanthemum fair can last from a few days to more than ten days where the main activities include enjoying chrysanthemum, competing for the best chrysanthemum, composing poems in chrysanthemum themes, painting chrysanthemum, tasting chrysanthemum tea and performing chrysanthemum opera.

Xiaolan Chrysanthemum Fair reflects the typical Chinese chrysanthemum culture and has involved huge numbers of people and shows profound cultural connotation; therefore it has significant historical and cultural values. People admire the noble characters of chrysanthemum; therefore Xiaolan Chrysanthemum Fair has an important role for promoting cultural awareness, enhancing cultural exchange and building a harmonious society.

荔枝节 Lychee Festivals

荔枝原产于中国南部，与香蕉、菠萝、龙眼并称为"南国四大佳果"。广东省从化是著名的荔枝之乡，是中国荔枝生产基地之一。

广东省每年都会举行荔枝节，包括从化荔枝节、增城荔枝节、深圳荔枝节等。荔枝节期间，除了观赏、采摘、品尝荔枝之外，还举办歌舞表演、体育表演、美术摄影展、图书展览、商品展销、贸易洽谈等活动。增城最有名的荔枝是挂绿荔枝，成熟的挂绿荔枝外表红绿相间，有一条绿线贯穿果皮，而且果肉晶莹，爽脆香甜，是荔枝中的珍品，至今已经有 400 多年的历史。除增城挂绿之外，还有水晶球、糯米糍、桂味、妃子笑等品种。

荔枝非常适合产妇、老人、体质虚弱和病后调养的人。但是，有糖尿病或空腹时不适合吃荔枝。荔枝的核可以入药，治疗心气痛。但是，荔枝性热，吃太多容易上火，导致"荔枝病"，这时可以喝适量的凉茶或者用荔枝壳熬水喝去除火热。

Lychee originated from southern China, known as one of "Four Southern Fruit Delicacies", together with banana, pineapple and longan. The most well-known hometown of lychee is Conghua, Guangdong Province, which is one of the lychee production bases in China.

Lychee festivals are held every year in Guangdong, including Conghua Lychee Festival, Zengcheng Lychee Festival and Shenzhen Lychee Festival. During the lychee festival, activities include watching, picking-up and tasting lychees, and there are a number of organized dance shows, sports events, art festivals, book exhibitions, trade fairs and business meetings, etc. The most famous lychee from Zengcheng is "Gua Lü" (Green thread) lychee, with the skin of ripe lychee has red and green stripes, and noticeably there is a green line through the entire fruit. Its crystal flesh, crispy and sweet taste make it a precious species, which has enjoyed over 400 years of history. There are also other varieties, such as Crystal Ball, Nuomici, Guiwei, Feizixiao.

Lychee is especially suitable for new mothers, elderly people, weak patients and people in medical care. However, people with diabetes or in hunger should not eat lychee. The lychees' seeds can be used as a kind of herb medicine, for treatment of heart, etc. However, lychee is rich in heat (a Chinese belief), so eating too much will accumulate "inner heat", resulting in "lychee illness". In this case, one needs to drink some herbal tea or lychee shell tea to remove the "inner heat".

龙舟赛 Dragon Boat Racing

龙舟赛是中国端午节（农历五月初五）的主要习俗之一，至今已经有2000多年的历史，在中国南方很流行。

龙舟是一种形状像龙、长十四五米的船。龙舟一般比较窄小，只能容纳两个人并排坐下。赛龙舟时，一般由20~30名队员组成一支参赛队伍，分两排坐在龙舟中间，每人手拿一支船桨用力向前划行，船头一名队员手拿彩旗进行指挥，船尾一名队员充当鼓手，用力擂鼓，控制节奏、鼓舞士气。

10 广东民俗
Guangdong Folk Traditions

Dragon boat racing is one of the main events of the Chinese Dragon Boat Festival (the fifth of May in Chinese lunar calendar). It has more than 2,000 years of history and is very popular in southern China.

The dragon boat is in the shape of a dragon, normally about fifteen meters long. Dragon boats are normally narrow and can only accommodate two people side by side, in rows, sitting down. During the dragon boat racing, there are about 20−30 players on a team, sitting in the dragon boat in two rows, each holding a paddle and rowing forward with great efforts. One player on the bow holds a coloured flag to give instructions to the team members, while another player on the stern beats a drum hard for controlling the rhythm and boosting morale.

广东省潮汕地区有很多江河,每年端午节都会举行龙舟赛,吸引着千家万户沿江观看。潮汕的龙舟一般有龙头、龙颈、龙尾。龙身是半圆形,宽1.4~1.6m,长短不一,可以容纳12对桨、16对桨、32对桨,甚至52对桨。龙舟分红龙、黄龙、青龙、白龙,由于乌龙被认为容易出事,人们不使用。龙身和龙腹涂成彩色鳞甲的样子,一般还挂有不同颜色的长龙须,鲜艳醒目。

龙舟赛来源于一个传说,相传古时候的楚国人因为舍不得贤臣屈原投江死去,许多人争先恐后划船去救他,但是,追了很远也不见踪迹。从此以后,每年农历五月初五,人们都会划龙舟进行纪念,并借划龙舟驱散江中的鱼,以免吃掉屈原的遗体。如今,龙舟赛已经演变为中国民间传统水上体育娱乐项目,成为2010年广州亚洲运动会正式比赛项目。

Since there are plenty of rivers in Chaoshan area, Guangdong Province, dragon boat racing becomes an annual event on Dragon Boat Festival, attracting thousands of people along the river to watch. Dragon boats in Chaoshan area commonly have a dragon head, dragon neck and dragon tail. Its body is in the shape of a semicircle with varying lengths and a width of 1.4−1.6 meters. The capacity of a boat can be up to 12 pairs of oars, 16 pairs of oars, 32 pairs of oars and even 52 pairs of oars. Dragon boats normally are red dragon, yellow dragon, green dragon and white dragon. Black dragons are rarely used because it is believed that they are easy to overturn. The main body and belly of the dragon boats are painted in colourful dragon scales and some of them also have long colourful beards which are bright and eye-catching.

According to legend, the dragon boat racing comes from a story in the Kingdom of Chu in ancient times. There was a beloved official called Qu Yuan who threw himself into a river because his kingdom was occupied by enemy forces. People tried to rescue him and sailed up and down to look for him, but all the efforts were in vain. Since then, on the fifth day of May in lunar calendar each year, people will use dragon boats to commemorate him with a wish that the dragon boats will chase the fishes away in the river, so as Qu Yuan's body would not be eaten by them. Today, dragon boat racing has evolved into the Chinese folk traditional water sports entertainment, becoming an official event in 2010 Guangzhou Asian Games.

皮影戏 Pi Ying Play

皮影戏,以前叫"影子戏""灯影戏",用灯光照射兽皮或纸板做成的人物剪影,表演故事,是世界上最早由人配音的活动影画艺术,幕影演出原理、艺术表现手段等对电影的发明起到先导作用,有人认为皮影戏是"电影始祖"。

皮影戏发源于陕西省华县,清朝时期达到鼎盛,至今已经有2000多年的历史。表演时,艺人在白色幕布后面,一边操纵木偶人物,一边用当地流行的曲调唱述故事,同时配以打击乐器和弦乐。中国很多地方戏曲剧种都是从皮影戏中衍生出来的。

陆丰皮影戏的影人、影景都用牛皮做成,影人高约六寸,五官轮廓分明,四肢比例和真人类似。影窗长四尺,宽不足三尺,用杉木或者毛竹作窗框,窗户中间糊有白纸或者罩着白布。用汽灯作光源,以提高影像的清晰度。往往一两个人负责表演全部角色。其中最有特色的是旦角的构造,旦角的两臂都用布帛制成,动作柔和、多变。

陆丰皮影戏著名的剧目有四大连戏:《高文举连》《祝英台连》《秦雪梅连》《吕碧英连》。陆丰皮影戏具有很高的历史价值、艺术价值和教育价值。

10 广东民俗
Guangdong Folk Traditions

Pi Ying Play, formally called "Shadow Play" or "Light Shadow Show", is a kind of folk drama or play that uses puppets made of animal skins or cardboard as silhouettes of lights on backdrops or screens and the plays normally use historic or folk stories as themes. It is one of the earliest forms of movie art in the world with actual voices. The methods of screen performance and artistic expression are the roots of modern movies so that the Pi Ying Play is considered to be the "ancestor of film".

Pi Ying Play originated from Huaxian County, Shaanxi Province, and reached its peak during the Qing Dynasty. It has more than 2,000 years of history. During the show, the actors stay behind a white curtain and manipulate puppet characters, narrate stories by singing local popular songs and also by playing music using percussion and string instruments. Many Chinese operas are actually derivatives of Shadow Play.

The figures and scenes of Lufeng Pi Ying Play are normally made with leather, and the figures are typically about six inches tall, with lively facial features, and in proportion to a real human person. The show stage window is about four feet long and three feet wide; the window frames are made of wood or bamboo and the window screen uses white paper or cloth. Gas lamps are the source of light which give clear images on the screen. In most cases only one or two actors are responsible for all roles. One of the most distinctive characters is Dan (female role), and both of her arms are made with cloth which produce various gentle movements.

Lufeng Pi Ying Play has four well-known operas which are "Gao Wenju", "Zhu Yingtai", "Qin Xuemei" and "Lü Biying". Lufeng Pi Ying Play has added great values to historical study, art, and education.

醒狮 Lion Dance

醒狮，属于中国狮舞中的南狮，由唐朝的宫廷狮子舞演变而来，发源于广东省南海县。广东醒狮被认为是驱邪避害的吉祥瑞物，因此节庆或者重大活动时都有醒狮表演，在广东、广西及东南亚等地比较流行。

醒狮融武术、舞蹈、音乐等为一体。醒狮有一些固定的动作和套路，完全采用南拳武功的步法。这些动作刚劲有力，步法稳固。一般认为，学舞醒狮的人必须先学南拳，打好基础。醒狮的表演模仿狮子的动作，如出洞、下山、过桥、饮水、采青、醉睡、醉醒、上山、玩球等。其中"采青"是醒狮的精髓，有起、承、转、合等过程，具有戏剧性和故事性。还通过在地面或桩阵上的腾、挪、闪、扑、回旋、飞跃等动作，表现狮子的喜、怒、哀、乐、动、静、惊、疑等情态。

醒狮有音乐伴奏，主要乐器有鼓、锣等，音乐伴奏根据醒狮舞的不同动作和套路而设置，或快或慢，或强或弱，形成锣鼓喧天、上下腾飞的气势。

醒狮的种类有金狮、黑狮、红狮、彩狮。金狮用于迎宾或者隆重的交往礼仪，一般很少见。黑狮、红狮、彩狮分别代表不同的性格，黑狮代表凶猛，红狮代表稳重，彩狮代表温和。

10 广东民俗
Guangdong Folk Traditions

Originated in the Nanhai County, Guangdong Province, lion dance evolved from the palace lion dance in the Tang Dynasty, and it is classified as the southern Chinese lion dance. Guangdong lion dance has served as a lucky symbol for avoiding evil and harmful things. During festivals or in case of a major event, lion dance is a "must have" performance, and it is very popular in Guangdong, Guangxi and Southeast Asian countries.

The lion dance is a performance that combines martial arts, dance and music as a whole. It has fixed routines and movements; adopted the footwork of martial arts such as Nan Quan (a local school of martial art). These movements are powerful and strong with steady footwork. It is believed that one must first learn Nan Quan, laying in a solid foundation, prior to learning the lion dance. Lion dance mimics the movements of the lion, such as going out of the cave and downhill, crossing the bridge, drinking water, picking-up flower, being drunk in sleep and awakening, climbing mountain or playing with a ball. Among the above mentioned is the "picking-up flower" as the best, and there are a series of movements of starting, following, transiting and ending, providing four stages of dramatic effect. This is especially true when performing movements of standing, stepping, flashing, fluttering, swing, leaping, and others on ground or pile array, showing lion's joy, anger, sadness, happiness, activeness, stillness, surprising, suspecting.

The lion dance is performed with music, drums, gongs and other musical instruments. The music is designed to support the lion dance routines, fast or slow, heavy or light, creating an atmosphere with loud drum and gong beats and upper and downward movement of the lion dance.

Types of lion include golden lion, black lions, red lions and color lions. The golden lions are used for special occasions, such as meeting important guests or holding a diplomatic ceremony, which are rarely seen. Black, red and colorful lions represent different personalities—the black lion for being ferocious, red lion for being stable while the color lion for being mild and tender.

11 广东风景名胜

Guangdong Scenic Resorts

白云山 Baiyun Mountain

白云山景色秀丽,自古以来就是广州有名的风景胜地。

白云山一共有七个游览区,其中包括:中国最大的园林式花园——云台花园,最大的天然鸟笼——鸣春谷,最大的雕塑主题公园——雕塑公园。云台花园以加拿大布查特花园为蓝本,聚东西方园林建筑精华于一体。鸣春谷包括鸟类标本陈列室、大型鸟笼景区、珍稀鸟展区、驯鸟表演区等,放养的鸟类150多种,共5000多只,广州人把它叫作"小鸟天堂"。

白云山有植物870多种,绿化覆盖率达95%以上,绿化面积2800公顷,每天可吸收2800多吨二氧化碳,释放2100多吨氧气,可供近300万人正常呼吸之用,被称为广州市的"市肺"。据测定,白云山的空气质量已达国家一级标准,噪声质量达国家0类标准,地表水质也达到国际规定,一些山涧水、泉水甚至可以直接饮用。

到了周末或者节假日,广州人喜欢去爬白云山。每年2~3月份,白云山桃花涧的桃花开得非常灿烂,广州人以看桃花祈求桃花运,即在事业、学业、爱情等方面的好运。

11 广东风景名胜
Guangdong Scenic Resorts

Baiyun Mountain has beautiful landscapes, and it is one of the most well-known resorts in Guangzhou even dating back to ancient times.

There are in total seven site-seeing areas in Baiyun Mountain, which include China's largest landscape garden—Yuntai Garden; the largest natural bird sanctuary—Mingchun (Singing Spring) Valley; and the largest sculptured theme park—Sculpture Park. Yuntai Garden uses Butchart Gardens in Canada as a blueprint and combines the best characters of Eastern and Western gardens and architectures. Mingchun Valley comprises bird specimen showrooms, large numbers of caged birds, exhibitions of rare birds and performance areas of tame birds. There are more than 150 varieties of birds and over 5,000 birds. Cantonese call the valley as the "birds' paradise".

There are more than 870 types of plants in the Baiyun Mountain area and more than 95% of the area is covered by green plants, which is equaled to 2,800 hectares. It is said that the plants can absorb more than 2,800 tonnes of carbon dioxide and produce more than 2,100 tonnes of oxygen, which is enough for about 3 million people so that the mountain is called "Lung of Guangzhou City". According to official measurements, the air quality of Baiyun Mountain has reached the national grade one standard; the noise level is also below the national limit; surface water quality meets international standards; and water from some streams and springs are directly drinkable.

During weekends or holidays, Cantonese like to climb Baiyun Mountain. During February and March of each year, peach flowers bloom magnificently in the "Peach Valley" of Baiyun Mountain, and the locals are very keen to watch the flowers and wish for good luck in work, education, love, etc.

丹霞山 Danxia Mountain

世界上的丹霞地貌主要分布在中国、美国西部、中欧和澳大利亚等地，在中国分布最广。其中丹霞山面积最大、类型最齐全、风景最优美。

丹霞山是世界"丹霞地貌"的命名地。丹霞山风景区包括上、中、下三层，上层景区有长老峰、海螺峰、宝珠峰、阳元山、阴元山。长老峰上建有一座御风亭，可以同时容纳200多人观看日出。海螺峰顶有螺顶浮屠，附近有许多相思树。宝珠峰有虹桥拥翠、舵石朝曦、龙王泉等景点。阳元山、阴元山分别有形似男性和女性生殖器的石头。中层景区以别传寺为主，从这里通过合掌一般狭窄的岩石，可以到达通天峡。下层景区主要有锦岩洞天胜景，在天然岩洞内有观音殿、大雄宝殿，还有一块颜色随四季而变化的"龙鳞片石"，非常有名。

丹霞山还有800多处石窟寺遗址、历代文人墨客留下的传奇故事、诗词和摩崖石刻，具有极大的历史文化价值。

丹霞山的最佳旅行时间是每年3~5月以及10~12月。

11 广东风景名胜
Guangdong Scenic Resorts

Danxia Land form around the world are mainly located in China, the western United States, central Europe, and Australia; however most of them are in China. Among them, Danxia Mountain has the largest area, most complete varieties of land formations and most typical and most beautiful view.

Danxia Landforms are named after Danxia Mountain. Danxia Mountain scenic area includes three areas from lower to higher ranges. In the upper area, there are "Zhanglao (Senior Monk) Peak", "Hailuo (Conch) Peak", "Baozhu (Precious Pearl) Peak", "Yang Yuan Mountain" and "Yin Yuan Mountain". There is a pavilion named Yufeng (Royal Wind) on top of the Zhanglao Peak, which can accommodate more than 200 people for watching the sunrise. On the top of Conch Peak there is a dagoba named Luoding Futu with many acacia trees nearby. There are a number of resorts in the Baozhu Peak area, such as "Hong Qiao Yong Cui (Rainbow on Green Woods)", "Duo Shi Zhao Xi (Stone Rudder in Dawn)", and "Long Wang Quan (Dragon King Spring)". Yang Yuan Mountain and Yin Yuan Mountain have huge rocks look like male and female genitals respectively. In the middle area, it is mainly the Biechuan Temple; there is a very narrow path through the rocks reaching "Tong Tian Xia". The lower area has "Jin Yan Dong Tian (Cave Attractions)", which has natural caves called the Guanyin Buddha Hall and Main Hall, and there is also a well-known rock called "Long Lin Pian Shi (meaning dragon scales)" which can change colours with the seasons.

Danxia Mountain also has more than 800 relics of cave temple, legend, historical stories, poetry and stone carving with great historical and cultural values.

The best time visiting Danxia Mountain is between March and May as well as between October and December.

鼎湖山 Dinghu Mountain

鼎湖山位于北纬 23°10′，东经 112°31′。因为地球上北回归线穿过的地方大都是沙漠或者干草原，所以鼎湖山又被中外学者誉为"北回归线上的绿宝石"。鼎湖山与丹霞山、罗浮山、西樵山合称"广东省四大名山"。

鼎湖山面积 1133 公顷，最高处的鸡笼山顶高 1000.3 米，从山麓到山顶依次分布着沟谷雨林、常绿阔叶林、亚热带季风常绿阔叶林等森林类型。鼎湖山因为特殊的研究价值而闻名海内外，被誉为华南生物种类的"基因储存库"和"活的自然博物馆"。

鼎湖山自唐代以来就是著名的佛教圣地和旅游胜地。公元 676 年，惠能的弟子智常禅师在鼎湖山建成白云寺，从此以后，高僧云集。明朝崇祯年间，鼎湖山上建成莲花庵，第二年重建山门，改称庆云寺。

鼎湖山宝鼎园中有一个大鼎，名叫九龙宝鼎，高 6.68 米，口径 5.58 米，重 16 吨，是世界上最大的鼎。口沿下有三组对称的龙纹，共六条龙，加上三足顶端有三个大龙头，共有九条龙。龙是中华民族的象征，九是最大数，九龙寓意深刻。大鼎的腹部有波曲纹，回环曲折，好像层峦叠嶂，寓意大地山川充满生机。

11 广东风景名胜
Guangdong Scenic Resorts

Dinghu Mountain is located at 23°10′N, 112°31′E. Because the most of places on the earth passing through the Tropic of Cancer are either deserts or dry grasslands, Dinghu Mountain is regarded as "An Emerald on the Tropic of Cancer" by scholars from home and abroad. Dinghu Mountain, together with Danxia Mountain, Luofu Mountain, Xiqiao Mountain, are known as the four famous mountains in Guangdong Province.

Dinghu Mountain has an area of 1,133 hectares. The highest peak is Jilong which is 1,000.3 meters high. From the foothills to the top there are distributed different types of forests, such as ravine rain forest, evergreen broad-leaved forest and subtropical monsoon evergreen broad-leaved forest. Because of its special research values, Dinghu Mountain is known as the "Genetic Repository" and "Living Natural Museum of South China", hence it has become very well-known worldwide.

Dinghu Mountain has been famous since the Tang Dynasty as a Buddhist shrine and a tourist resort. In 676A.D., the disciple of Huineng, Zhi Chang, built Baiyun Temple on Dinghu Mountain, and there have been many great monks who lived here since then. During Chongzhen year in the Ming Dynasty, Lotus Temple was built on the top of the mountain, and then renamed Qingyun Temple after the renovation of the main gate the following year.

There is a giant tripod, named Kowloon Baoding (Nine Dragons Treasure Tripod), in Baoding Park of Dinghu Mountain, which is 6.68 meters high, 5.58 meters in diameter and weighs 16 tones. It is the largest tripod in the world. Under the rim, there are six dragons, three pairs in symmetry; there is also a dragon on each of three feet, making it nine dragons in total. The dragon is a symbol of the Chinese nation and nine is the largest single digit number, therefore nine dragons have a profound meaning. In the middle of the giant tripod, there are engraved wave patterns, with endless twists and turns, like boundless rising peaks resembling the land,which means that mountains and rivers are full of vitality.

黄埔军校 Whampoa Military Academy

黄埔军校,建校时的正式名称是中国国民党陆军军官学校,后来改为中华民国陆军军官学校。因为校址设在广东省广州市东南方的黄埔岛上,历史上称为黄埔军校。

黄埔军校是孙中山先生在中国共产党和苏联的积极支持下创办的第一所培养革命干部的新型军事政治学校。在中国现代历史上影响深远、作用巨大、声名显赫。

黄埔军校的首任校长是蒋介石。军校在黄埔岛上办到第七期,1930年9月迁往南京,后来又迁往成都和台湾。

Whampoa Military Academy got its name because the school site was located on Whampoa Island in the southeast of Guangzhou City, Guangdong Province. Its former official name was Chinese Nationalist Party (KMT) Military Academy, and it was later renamed the Republic of China Military Academy.

The Whampoa Military Academy was a new type of military-political school, to train revolutionary cadres, founded by Sun Yat-sen with the support of the Communist Party of China (CPC) and the Soviet Union. It had great and profound impacts on modern Chinese history.

The first president of the Whampoa Military Academy was Chiang Kai-shek. The school had seven training sessions on the island, and then was moved to Nanjing in September of 1930 and was later moved to Chengdu and Taiwan.

黄埔岛在珠江的中央,这里树木成荫、环境清幽,非常适合学习和练武。黄埔军校的四周修筑有围墙,建筑面积1060平方米。军校主体建筑是一幢走马楼,这是一座岭南祠堂式四合院建筑,砖木结构,一共有两层,有三条走廊把四排房屋连接起来,以南北走向的中轴线为中心,呈东西对称分布。黄埔军校设有政治、教授、训练、管理、军需、军医等六个部,另外设有学员宿舍、食堂、展览室等。1938年,在抗日战争中,被日本战机炸毁。1996年,完成重建并对外开放。

军校大门西边有一幢两层砖木结构的房屋,孙中山曾于民国六年(1917年)在这里居住。1984年,改建为黄埔军校纪念馆,展示军校校史和孙中山在广东进行革命活动时的照片。军校南边的八卦山上建有孙中山纪念碑。

11 广东风景名胜
Guangdong Scenic Resorts

Whampoa Island is located in the centre of Pearl River, which is a wooded area with a quiet environment, and it is an ideal location for military education. Whampoa Military Academy is enclosed by high walls and has a floor area of 1,060 square meters. The main building is a Zouma Lou, which is a type of Lingnan ancestral temple courtyard building, and there are two storeys made of bricks and wood, four rows of houses are connected by three corridors. The layout is symmetrical on the east and west sides with a north-south centre axis. The Whampoa Military Academy has six departments, namely Politics, Education, Practice, Management, Military Supplies and Military Medicine, and there are also student dormitories, dining halls and exhibition rooms. The building was destroyed during Japanese bombing in 1938, during the Chinese People's War of Resistance against Japanese Aggression. The current building was completely rebuilt and opened to public in 1996.

There is a two-storey brick house on the west of Military Academy door, and Dr. Sun Yat-sen lived there in 1917. It was converted to the Whampoa Military Academy Memorial in 1984, displaying the photos of the school's history and Sun Yat-sen's revolutionary activities in Guangdong. To the south of the Military Academy there is a Sun Yat-sen Monument on top of Bagua Hill.

李小龙乐园 Bruce Lee Theme Park

世界著名武打巨星李小龙的祖居在广东省佛山市顺德区均安镇，李小龙乐园就建在这里。园内湖泊连绵、绿树成荫、环境清幽，称得上是珠三角的"世外桃源"。

李小龙纪念馆是李小龙乐园的主体建筑，也是目前世界上最大的李小龙纪念馆，占地面积3000多平方米。主题"印象李小龙"全面展现功夫之王的传奇一生，共分十个篇章，以十个独立的展厅进行展示。这里矗立着世界上最高的李小龙铜像，铜像高12米，基座高6米，总高度18米。乐园内建有仿制的李小龙祖居，祖居是李小龙的祖父和父亲曾经居住过的地方，是民国初年的建筑风格，青砖碧瓦，古朴典雅。

李小龙乐园是"顺德新十景"之一，深受全球"龙迷"的喜爱。

11 广东风景名胜
Guangdong Scenic Resorts

The hometown of worldwide well-known martial art star Bruce Lee was in Jun'an Town, Shunde District, Foshan City, Guangdong. Bruce Lee Theme Park (Bruce Lee Paradise) is built there, and the park has lakes and woods creating a quiet and serene environment. It is a "paradise" in the Pearl River Delta area.

Bruce Lee Memorial Hall is the main building of the Bruce Lee Theme Park, which is currently the world's largest Bruce Lee memorial hall covering an area of over 3,000 square meters. The theme of "Impression of Bruce Lee" comprehensively displays the legendary life of the King of Kung Fu, and it consists of 10 titles and exhibits in 10 individual halls. There stands the world's tallest bronze statue of Bruce Lee, which is 12 meters high with a 6-meter high base, and the total height is 18 meters. There in the park is built an imitation of Bruce Lee's ancestral home, where Bruce Lee's father and grandfather had lived. It is an architectural style of the early Republic, with glazed tiles and bricks, and it is traditional but elegant.

The Bruce Lee Theme Park is one of the "Ten Best Shunde New Resorts", and it is beloved by fans of Bruce Lee worldwide.

罗浮山 Luofu Mountain

罗浮山位于广东省惠州市博罗县西北部,又叫东樵山,和位于佛山市境内的西樵山是姐妹山,是中国道教①十大名山之一,有"岭南第一山"的美誉。

罗浮山以草药闻名于世。东晋年间,著名道教理论家、炼丹家、医学家葛洪在罗浮山中修建道观,采药济世,修道炼丹,著书立说,写成《抱朴子·内篇》一书,确定了中国的神仙理论体系,丰富了道教的思想内容。北宋诗人苏东坡在这里写下"罗浮山下四时春,卢桔杨梅次第新。日啖荔枝三百颗,不辞长作岭南人"的名句,罗浮山从此闻名天下。

①道教发源于古代中国,是一种传统的多神宗教,追求得道成仙、救济世人。老子的《道德经》是最主要的经典。

Luofu Mountain is located in the northwest area of Huizhou City, Guangdong Province, also known as Dongqiao Mountain which is the sister Mountain of Xiqiao Mountain located in Foshan City. It is one of the top ten famous mountains of Taoism [1] in China and has a reputation as the "Number One Mountain in Lingnan".

Luofu Mountain is well known for its richness in herbs. Ge Hong, who was a famous Taoist theorist, alchemist and medical physician in the Eastern Jin Dynasty, lived on Luofu Mountain. He built Taoist temples, made Chinese herb medicines for patients, practiced Taoist religion. He wrote books and one of the most important works was *Bao Puzi • Inner Chapters*, which became the foundation of Chinese mythology theories and enriched Taoist thoughts. The well-known poet Su Dongpo in the Northern Song Dynasty wrote a famous poem on Luofu Mountain, which goes, "Spring the only season in Luofu, one after another bayberries and loquats bloom, three hundred lychees my daily taste, living in Lingnan and staying without haste." Since then Luofu Mountain has become very well-known in China.

---

① Originated in ancient China, Taoism is a traditional polytheistic religion. It advocates immortal life and relief to the world. *Tao Te Ching* by Lao Tzu is the most important classic book.

罗浮山的特色景观有奇峰、飞瀑和洞天。有432座山峰,著名的有飞云峰、铁桥峰、玉女峰、骆驼峰、上界峰等。其中飞云峰是主峰,海拔1281米,高耸入云。有980多处飞瀑,著名的有白漓瀑布、白水门瀑布、黄龙洞瀑布、白莲湖、芙蓉池、长生井等。有朱明、蓬莱、桃源、蝴蝶、夜乐等18个大洞天,其中朱明洞是山上最大的洞穴。

罗浮山处在北回归线上,属亚热带季风气候,雨量充足,植物垂直分布变化明显。山上生长着1200多种药用植物和各种水果,形成了独特的罗浮山特产,有罗浮山百草油、酥醪菜、云雾甜茶等。

去罗浮山可以看日出、日落、游云和大海,非常漂亮。

11 广东风景名胜
Guangdong Scenic Resorts

The beautiful landscapes of Luofu Mountain consist of unique peaks, waterfalls and caves. There are in total 432 peaks, including the famous Flying Cloud Peak, Iron Bridge Peak, Fairy Lady Peak, Camel Peak and Shang Jie (Heaven) Peak. Among them, the Flying Cloud Peak is the main one measuring 1,281 meters high above sea level, almost as tall as clouds. Also on the mountain areas there are more than 980 waterfalls, with the more famous ones being Bai Li Falls, White Watergate Falls, Yellow Dragon Cave Falls, White Lotus Lake, Hibiscus Pond and Long Live Well. There are 18 caves and the notable ones are Zhu Ming (Scarlet and Bright), Peng Lai (Mirage), Tao Yuan (Peach Valley), Hu Die (Butterflies) and Ye Yue (Night Music), and among them the Zhu Ming is the biggest.

Luofu Mountain is close to the Tropic of Cancer with a subtropical monsoon climate. There are sufficient rainfall, and the varieties of plant change significantly from the foot to the top of the mountain. There grow more than 1,200 kinds of medical herb plant and a variety of fruits in the mountain, and they are unique special of Luofu Mountain, such as, Bai Cao Oil, Crisp Fermented Vegetables, Sweet Tea, etc.

On the top of Luofu Mountain one could watch sunrise, sunset, floating clouds and the sea, which are magnificent and beautiful sceneries.

西樵山 Xiqiao Mountain

古西樵山人创造了灿烂的"双肩石器"文明,被称为"珠江文明的灯塔"。明清时期,大批文人学子隐居在这里,所以又称"南粤理学名山"。西樵山也是"南拳文化"的发源地,一代武术宗师黄飞鸿①就诞生在西樵山附近的村落。

西樵山位于广东省佛山市南海区的西南部,以儒、佛、道三教融合为特色。

字祖庙供奉着汉字创造者仓颉,奎光楼供奉着魁星②神。字祖庙和奎光楼都建于清乾隆丁酉年间(1777年)。当时的西樵学子参加科举考试都难以金榜题名。为了振兴文气,由西樵简村的大户人家捐资修建。建好后,每逢学子进京赶考、孩童入学启蒙,都要来这里跪拜,祈求好运。

---

①黄飞鸿(1847—1924),广东南海西樵禄舟村人,洪拳大师,也是救死扶伤的名医。传世拳术套路有工字伏虎拳、虎鹤双形拳、铁线拳、五形拳等。

②魁星,是中国古代一个星宿的名称,也是一个神话人物,主宰文运,在儒士学子心目中具有至高无上的地位。

Ancient people in Xiqiao Mountain created a splendid civilization of "the Shoulders Neolithic" which is regarded as "Beacon of the Pearl River Civilization". During the Ming and Qing Dynasties, a large number of scholars and students lived on Xiqiao Mountain, so it is also called "the Scholar Mountain of Nan Yue (southern Guangdong)". It is also the birthplace of martial arts Nan Quan and master Wong Fei-hung[①] was born in a village near Xiqiao Mountain.

Xiqiao Mountain is located in the southwest of the Nanhai District of Foshan City, Guangdong Province, and it has a special mixture of culture from Confucianism, Buddhism and Taoism.

The Zizu (Father of Chinese Characters) Temple is dedicated to the Chinese characters' creator Cang Jie, and Kuiguang Tower to the God Kui Xing[②]. The Zizu Temple and Kuiguang Tower were built in the Qianlong Ding You year (1777) during the Qing Dynasty. In those years, the Xiqiao students took part in the imperial examinations but found it difficult to pass. In order to revitalize the literary ambience, the rich families from Jian Village around Xiqiao donated to build the Zizu Temple and the Kuiguang Tower. Since then, students who needed to go the capital city (Beijing) for examinations or children who were about to attend school, must go there to worship and pray for good luck.

---

① Wong Fei-hung(1847-1924), from Qiaoluzhou Village, Nanhai, Guangdong, master of Hongquan (Hong Fist), also a popular doctor. His masterpiece of inherited martial art included Gong Zi Fu Hu Fist, Hu He Shuang Xing Fist, Tie Xian Fist and Wu Xing Fist.

② Kui Xing is a God of Chui Star in Chinese ancient myth, who ruled the fortune of intelligence, had a paramount position in hearts of scholars.

世界第一观音坐像就矗立在西樵第二高峰大仙峰上,观音像高61.9米,寓意观音在6月19日成道。观音像莲花座直径36米,莲花座内部是一个五层大厅,陈列着许多观音文化艺术品。莲花座四面环水,有四桥通达,寓意四方净土,八方德水。大仙峰左侧建有具有很高艺术价值的国内外观音寺庙、观音造像微缩景区。此外,还有圣域市肆、福寿莲池、环海镜清、牌坊广场等观音文化建筑群。

西樵山黄大仙①圣境园集道教文化、岭南建筑艺术和自然景观于一体,是祈福朝圣的道教圣地。园区尽头石壁下有高28米的黄大仙圣像,圣像坐西北朝东南,手持拂尘,身披道袍,慈祥肃穆,仙风道骨。

①黄大仙(约328—386年),原名黄初平,浙江省金华市人,著名的道教神仙。后人把他奉为掌管财运的神灵,很受欢迎。

On the top of the second highest peak in Xiqiao Mountain, Da xian Peak, there stands the world's number one Guanyin (one of Buddha, Goddess of Mercy) sculpture, which is 61.9 meters tall, and she was enlightened (passed away in Buddhism) on June 19th. The lotus seat of the sculpture has a diameter of 36 meters, and there is a five-storey hall inside; a large

number of art works of the Guanyin Culture are also displayed. The lotus seat is surrounded by a pond, accessible by four bridges, meaning the "Pure Land of Four Aspects and Virtuous Water in Eight Directions". On the left side of the Daxian Peak, there was built a miniature scenic area of Guanyin Temples from home and abroad, which is very attractive. In addition, there are many other Guanyin cultural buildings including Sheng Yu Shi Si (Holy Land and Towns), Fu Shou Lian Chi (Good Fortune and Long Life Lotus Pool), Huan Hai Jing Qing (Sea Coast Clear Mirror), Wong Tai Sin and Pai Fang (Memorial Arch) Square,etc.

Wong Tai Sin [①] Sacred Garden, is a combination of Taoism, Lingnan architecture and natural landscapes and is the holy land for Taoism pilgrimages. At the bottom of the garden, there is a sculpture of Wong Tai Sin under the stone wall. The sculpture sits facing southeast, holding a long whisk, wearing a Taoist robe, and he looks kind and powerful like a god.

---

① Wong Tai Sin, original name Huang Chuping, from Jinhua City, Zhejiang province, a well known Taoist. People worship him as the God of Fortune, hence very popular.

12 广东文化名人

Guangdong Celebrities

陈献章 Chen Xianzhang

陈献章（1428—1500）是广东省江门市新会区人，明代"心学"大师、教育家、书法家、诗人。主张学习重在提出疑问，进而独立思考，提倡自由开放的学风，逐渐形成一个有自己特点的学派——江门学派。因为曾经在白沙村居住，人称白沙先生。有"广东第一大儒"的盛誉。

在陈献章出生前，他的父亲就去世了，母亲独自抚养他，还要操持家事。陈献章小时候体弱多病，特殊的家庭环境，使陈献章对母亲特别孝顺。

长大后的陈献章专心读书，足不出户。为了减少对他的干扰，家人就在墙壁上凿了一个洞，饮食衣服，都从洞口进出。经过十年苦学，陈献章的学问与修养有了巨大进步。1465年春季，陈献章设馆教学，学生慕名而来，门庭若市。陈献章的教学方法与众不同，主张先静坐、后读书，多自学、少灌输，勤思考、取精义，重疑问、求真知。除了教授经史文学等课程外，他注重实际，课余时间常常和学生到旷野去练习骑马射箭。

陈献章留存各种体裁的诗作有1977首，他的诗文著述由他的学生编辑成《白沙子全集》出版传世。陈献章的书法自成一家，习惯用自制的"茅龙"笔（用硬朗的茅草制成）写字，字体苍劲有力，别具风格。

12 广东文化名人
Guangdong Celebrities

Chen Xianzhang (1428–1500), native of Xinhui District, Jiangmen City, Guangdong Province, was a master of the "Mind" school during the Ming Dynasty and was an educator, calligrapher and poet. He advocated "studying unknowns is a valuable element in the process of learning", and "independent thinking". He also promoted free and open style of study and gradually formed a method of his own characteristics called the Jiangmen School. Because once lived in Baisha Village, he was also known as Mr. Bai Sha, and he had a reputation of being the "Number One Confucius Scholar in Guangdong".

Chen Xianzhang's father died before giving birth of a posthumous child. His mother had to raise the son and earn a living for the family. When he was little, Chen Xianzhang was weak and unhealthy. Because of the special family situation, he cared for his mother very much.

The young Chen Xianzhang focused on studying and rarely left home. In order to reduce the interference, his family dug a hole in the wall for providing him foods and clothes. After a decade of hard work, he made tremendous progress in learning and accomplishments. In the spring of 1465, Chen Xianzhang opened a school for teaching, and many students came with admiration. His teaching method was different, which was meditation first (sit down quietly to create a peaceful mind), then reading; more self studies, and less taught lessons, focusing on the essence of context, and re-doubting to seek the truth. Except teaching confucius books, history and literature courses, he also paid attentions to sporting practices. He often went in his spare time to practice horse riding and archery with his students.

He has 1,977 poems in total in various forms retained, and his poems and works were edited into a book called *The Complete Works of White Sand* by his students and then published. His calligraphy also stands out in a unique style as he usually used his home-made "Mao Dragon" pen (brush pen made from tough thatch) to write, and his writing was vigorous, strong and very stylish.

红线女 Hung Sin-nui

红线女(1924—2013)是广东省开平水口镇泮村人,花旦(中国传统戏曲的行当,青年或中年女性形象),著名粤剧表演艺术家,粤剧红派表演艺术创始人。

1938年红线女师从舅母何芙莲学戏,初起艺名小燕红。后来,同班著名艺人给她讲述了"红线盗盒"的侠义故事,因此自己改艺名为红线女。抗日战争时期,香港沦陷后,随马师曾的太平剧团在广东、广西各地演出。抗日战争胜利后,在中国广东、香港、澳门,越南,新加坡,马来西亚等地演出。1952年在香港组建真善美剧团。1955年回到广东后,先后主演了很多剧目,她所塑造的人物形象感情丰满、性格突出、深入人心,形成独具特色的"红派"表演艺术。许多"红腔"名曲至今仍广为传唱。

从艺60多年来,红线女演过近百个粤剧,拍过90多部电影。在继承粤剧传统的基础上,吸收、借鉴京剧、昆剧、话剧、歌剧、电影及西洋歌唱技巧,创造使海内外观众为之倾倒的"红腔",把粤剧旦角唱腔发展到一个崭新的阶段。代表作《荔枝颂》《珠江礼赞》《昭君出塞》成为粤剧唱腔的经典。粤剧因此被周恩来誉为"南国红豆"。2009年,红线女获首届"中国戏剧终身成就奖"。

12 广东文化名人
Guangdong Celebrities

Hung Sin-nui, born in 1924 in Pan Village, Shuikou Town, Kaiping City, Guangdong Province, was a Faa Daan (young or middle-aged women of the traditional Chinese opera), a famous Cantonese opera artist and the founder of the Red Faction of Cantonese Opera.

She started to learn drama from her aunt Ho Fulian in 1938 and had a stage name called Little Yanhong. Later she was renamed as Hung Sin-nui based on a story "Stolen Box by Hung Sin-nui" told by an artist from the same group. During the period of the Chinese People's War of Resistance against Japanese Aggression, after the fall of Hong Kong, she followed Taiping Troupe led by Ma Shizeng and performed in Guangdong and Guangxi Provinces. After the victory of the war, she performed in China's Guangdong, Hong Kong, Macao; Vietnam; Singapore; Malaysia and other areas. The Sound of Music Theatre Company was set up by her in Hong Kong in 1952. After returned to Guangdong in 1955, she starred in many plays, created a large number of popular, passionate and unique stage characters, and formed the unique "Red Faction" Performing Art. Today, many of the "Red Tone" music and songs are still widely sung.

During 60 years of performing, Ramble played nearly a hundred operas and starred in more than 90 films. Based on traditional Cantonese Opera, she absorbed and learned from the Peking Opera, Kunqu Opera, regular operas, films and Western singing skills. Then she created the "Red Tone" which was beloved by audiences at home and abroad, brought the Daan (female role) singing of Cantonese Opera to a higher level. Her masterpieces,*Lychee Song*,*Pearl River Praise* and *Lady Zhaojun*, have become classics of Cantonese Opera singing. Former Premier, Zhou Enlai, called Cantonese Opera a "Red Bean in Southern Country". Ramble received the first "Chinese Drama Lifetime Achievement Award" in 2009.

惠能 Hui Neng

惠能是中国唐代的高僧,中国佛教禅宗六祖,著有《六祖坛经》流传于世。与代表东方思想的孔子、老子合称"东方三圣人"。

在惠能小的时候,父亲去世,后来随母亲移居南海,以卖柴为生。一次,在卖柴回家的路上听到有人诵读《金刚经》中的"应无所住,而生其心"时,萌发学习佛法的想法。唐龙朔元年(公元661年),惠能前往湖北省黄梅县双峰山,拜谒禅宗五祖弘忍,五祖让他劈柴舂米八个多月。

当时的弘忍已经很老了,急于把衣钵传给弟子,就让弟子们各写一首偈。寺内高僧神秀写道:

身是菩提树,

心为明镜台,

时时勤拂拭,

勿使惹尘埃。

Hui Neng was one of the most respected monks of the Tang Dynasty, and he was the Sixth Patriarch of the Chinese Buddhist Zen Sect. His important works include The 6th Patriarch Platform Sutra. He is known as one of Three Oriental Prophets alongside with Confucius and Lao Tzu, who developed the traditional Chinese ideology.

His father passed away when Hui Neng was little. He then had to move and live in Nanhai with his mother selling firewood for living. One day, on the way back home from the market there was someone reading aloud the *Diamond Sutra*, and he suddenly had a wish to study Buddhism when he heard the quote "without being constrained by preconceived notions arising from the senses". In the Longsu First Year of the Tang Dynasty (661 A.D.), Hui Neng went to Shuangfeng Mountain, Huangmei County, Hubei Province and visited Hong Ren, the Fifth Patriarch of Chinese Buddhist Zen Sect. However, for more than eight months, Hong Ren only requested him to do some labour work, such as chopping firewood or grinding rice.

Hong Ren was old at that time and eager to choose a successor to inherit Insignia of the Patriarchate, so he asked every monk in the temple to write a verse. In the temple there was a senior monk named Shen Xiu, who wrote:

Let your body be a Buddhist tree,
And your mind a bright mirror.
And often clean them all over,
Then free from dust they will be.

意思是要时时刻刻照顾自己的心灵和心境,通过不断的修行来抗拒外界的诱惑。这是一种入世的心态,强调修行的作用。惠能也做了一首偈,请别人写在神秀的偈的旁边:

菩提本无树,

明镜亦非台,

本来无一物,

何处惹尘埃。

意思是世间万物都是空的,心本来也是空的,也就无所谓抗拒外界的诱惑,任何事物从心而过,不留痕迹。这是一种出世的态度,强调顿悟的理念。

弘忍将衣钵传给了惠能,并让他连夜逃走。惠能连夜远走南方,隐居10年之后,在曹溪宝林寺创立了禅宗的南宗。后来神秀成为梁朝的护国法师,创立了禅宗的北宗。

公元713年8月3日,六祖惠能大师圆寂,其真身塑像保存在广东省韶关市曲江区南华禅寺内。

It was to remind himself that attending to his soul and mind all the time in order to resist the temptations from the outside world. It stressed the importance of the Buddhism practices. Hui Neng also wrote a verse that was put side by side with that of Shen Xiu:

There is no Buddhist tree at all,
And there is bright mirror nor.
Now there is nothing at all,
How could be dust any more?

It means that everything in the world is actually nothing, including our minds; therefore there is no need to resist any kind of temptations, and all things passed through souls and minds without any trace. It emphasizes ideology of enlightenment.

Hong Ren passed over his Robe and the Alms Bowl to Hui Neng and advised him running away from the temple during the same night. Hui Neng then went to southern China and created the Southern Zen Sect in Baolin Temple located in Caoxi after ten years of hiding. At the same time, Shen Xiu also created the Northern Zen Sect while he was the Master of the Law of Liang Dynasty.

On August 3, 713 A.D. Sixth Patriarch Hui Neng passed away. The sculpture of his "real body" is kept in Nanhua Temple, Shaoguan City, Guangdong Province.

康有为 Kang Youwei

康有为（1858—1927）是广东南海人，人称"康南海"，是中国近代著名的学者、书法家、政治家、思想家和社会改革家，信奉孔子的儒家学说，致力于将儒家学说改造为可以适应中国现代社会的国教。

22岁那年在香港的游历，使康有为眼界大开。后来，他又阅读《海国图志》《瀛环志略》等书，从中学转为西学。1882年，康有为从北京回上海时，进一步接触到资本主义思想，收集很多介绍资本主义各国政治制度和自然科学的书刊。经过学习，康有为逐步认识到西方的资本主义制度比当时中国的封建制度先进，立志向西方学习，以挽救危亡中的中国。

12 广东文化名人
Guangdong Celebrities

Kang Youwei (1858–1927), from Nanhai, Guangdong Province, known as "Kang Nanhai", was a famous modern Chinese scholar, calligrapher, politician, thinker, and social reformer who believed in the Confucian doctrine and committed to the transformation of Confucianism so that it could be adapted as the state religion of China's modern society.

When Kang Youwei was 22-year-old, he travelled to Hong Kong and the trip opened his eyes. He read a lot books including like *The Illustrated Introduction to the Countries Oversea*, *Short Records of the World* etc., and then studied more Western works. In 1882, Kang Youwei went back to Shanghai from Beijing where he was further exposed to the ideology of capitalism and collected many books on political systems of the capitalistic countries and the natural sciences. He gradually realized that Western capitalism system was more advanced than China's feudal system so he was determined to learn from the West and to save China's perilous condition.

1895—1898年,康有为积极进行变法实践。1895年4月,康有为听说清政府要与日本签订丧权辱国的《马关条约》,极为愤慨,连夜起草了14000多字的上皇帝书。后来,康有为又连续给皇帝上了几次书。在这些上书中,康有为系统地阐述了自己的变法思想,从政治、经济、文化、教育等方面提出了自己的见解。提出变君主专制为君主立宪;发展工业,振兴商业,保护民族资产阶级利益;"开民智""兴学校""废八股"①。

1898年6月11日,变法正式开始。9月21日,慈禧太后发动政变,变法失败。前后一共103天,历史上称为百日维新。

---

①八股,又叫八股文,是中国明清考试制度所规定的一种特殊文体,只注重形式,不关心内容,文章的每个段落都必须遵守固定的格式,并且只能写固定的字数,严重束缚了作者的思想和表现力。

Between 1895 and 1898, Kang Youwei was actively practicing reforms. In April 1895, Kang Youwei heard the Qing Government decided to sign the humiliating *Treaty of Shimonoseki* with Japan and in extreme anger he on the same night drafted a proposal of 14,000 words to the Emperor. He went on to write many more proposals to the Emperor afterwards. Among these proposals, he systematically expounded the ideology of the reform and put forward his opinions from aspects of politics, economy, culture, education and other areas. He proposed changing the monarchy dictatorship to constitutional monarchy; promoted industrial developments including the revitalization of trade business and the protection of the national bourgeoisie interests, also policies on how to "improve intelligence of people", "set up more schools" and "abandon systems of Eight-Part Essay"[①].

His reform began on the 11th of June, 1898, but Empress Dowager Cixi launched a coup on the 21st of September and then the political reform failed. The reform lasted only 103 days, and therefore it is known as the "Hundred Days Reform" in Chinese history.

---

① Eight-Part Essay was a special format of articles and essays, regulated by the examination system in the Ming and Qing Dynasties, in which the most important factor was the format of the writing, but not the content. Every chapter and paragraph had a fixed format and fixed number of words. It greatly limited the writer's ability to express his or her thoughts and ideas.

李嘉诚 Li Ka-shing

李嘉诚（1928—　）出生在广东省潮州市。据2011年福布斯杂志的统计，李嘉诚的总资产值达260亿美元，再次成为全球华人的首富。

1939年，李嘉诚和家人来到香港，住在舅父家中。当时，李嘉诚的父亲得病去世，李嘉诚不得不结束学业，在舅父的公司当学徒，以维持一家人的生计。每天，他总是第一个到达公司，最后一个离开公司，并且学会了灵活处事。17岁时，李嘉诚在另一家公司当推销员，在推销的过程中，他学会了宽厚待人，为以后事业的发展打下了良好的基础。

为了学习相关技术，李嘉诚曾经以普通员工的身份进入意大利一家生产高档塑胶的公司工作。回国后，创建长江塑胶厂，生意火爆。

但是，由于产品供不应求，公司降低产品质量以应付订单。结果客户要求退货，银行追债，塑胶厂顿时陷入困境，濒临破产。有一天，母亲给李嘉诚讲了开元寺住持元寂和尚的一个故事，李嘉诚感触很深。后来，他用诚信打动银行、供货商和员工，形势因此好转。李嘉诚从此在商界站稳脚跟。

李嘉诚母亲讲的故事是这样的：元寂年事已高，希望在两个弟子（一寂和二寂）中选择一个做接班人。元寂分别给两个弟子一袋谷种，谁收获的谷子多，谁就是接班人。到第二年秋天，一寂挑来满满一担谷子，二寂则两手空空。元寂当众宣布二寂为接班人，因为二寂是诚实的。原来元寂给两个弟子的都是煮熟的谷子。

12 广东文化名人
Guangdong Celebrities

Li Ka-shing was born in 1928 in Chaozhou City, Guangdong Province. According to the *Forbes Magazine* 2011, Li Ka-shing had total assets valuing $ 26 billion and continued to be the richest Chinese in the world.

In 1939, Li Ka-shing went to Hong Kong with his family and lived with his uncle. At that time, his father became ill and passed away so he had to quit school and become an apprentice in the company, which was owned by his uncle, in order to make a living for the whole family. Every day, he was always the first one to arrive at work and the last one to leave, and he learned how to read people's faces and play things by ear. When he was 17-year old, Li Ka-shing became a salesman in another company and gradually learned the importance of generosity, which laid a good foundation for his future career development.

In order to master the techniques of making one type of Italian high-grade plastics, Li Ka-shing went to the chemical plant in Italy and worked as an ordinary employee. After returning home, he invested in the Yangtze River Plastics Plant, using the knowledge learned in Italy plant and established a profitable business.

Once, due to high demand, the company lowered product quality in order to meet the orders, which resulted in a huge number of refund claims from customers, and banks at the same time also asked for payment of debts, bringing the company to the brink of bankruptcy. One day his mother told him a story of Master Yuan Ji in Kaiyuan Temple, and Li Ka-shing was deeply moved by the story. Soon after, he convinced the banks, suppliers and employees with his honesty, and thus his financial situation became improved. Since then Li Ka-shing firmly stood in the business circle.

Here is the story told by Li Ka-shing's mother. As Master Yuan Ji became old, he wished to select a successor between two disciples (Yi Ji and Er Ji). Yuan Ji gave a sack of millet seed to each of the disciples and stated that whoever harvested more millet would be the successor. In autumn of the second year, Yi Ji came with a full load of millet, but Er Ji came back empty-handed. Yuan Ji then announced that Er Ji would become his successor for him being honest because the truth was that millet seeds they were given had already been cooked.

广东文化与社会

李小龙 Bruce Lee

李小龙 (1940—1973) 是武术宗师、无限制格斗锦标赛 (UFC) 起源者、综合格斗 (MMA) 之父、功夫影帝、功夫电影开创者、截拳道创始人、美国好莱坞首位华人演员。他革命性地推动了世界武术和功夫电影的发展,将"Kung Fu"一词写入了英文词典。美国人称他为功夫之王,日本人称他为武之圣者,泰国人称他为武打至尊。

李小龙生于美国三藩市,童年和少年在香港度过。幼时的李小龙身体非常瘦弱。为了使李小龙身体强壮,7岁时,他的父亲就教他练习太极拳,13岁时让他跟随叶问学习咏春拳。此外,练习螳螂拳、洪拳、少林拳、白鹤拳等拳种,参加西洋拳训练班,研究西洋拳的拳法,购买世界拳王路易斯的拳击赛纪录片,学习其步法、身法、拳法和训练方法。他还擅长长棍、短棍和双节棍等器械,经常参加拳击比赛,丰富实战经验。有一次,在美国佛罗里达州的唐人街,李小龙徒手制服4名持刀歹徒,救出华人少女。李小龙的名字随之传遍美国,中国功夫引起人们的重视。

Bruce Lee (1940—1973) was a martial arts master and one of the founders of the Ultimate Fighting Championship (UFC), father of the Mixed Martial Arts (MMA), king and pioneer of Kung Fu films, founder of Jeet Kune Do, and the first Chinese film actor in Hollywood in the United States of America. His contributions revolutionarily changed the development of the world of martial arts and Kung Fu films and even the term "Kung Fu" was written into English dictionaries. He was referred to as the King of Kung Fu in United States of America, also called the Warrior Saint in Japan, and known as Martial Arts Supreme in Thailand.

Bruce Lee was born in San Francisco, California, United States of America, and spent his childhood and youth in Hong Kong. He was very thin and weak as a child so in order to help him grow stronger, his father taught him to practice Tai Chi when he was seven years old and then later he learned Wing Chun from Master Ip Man at the age of 13. In addition, he also learned Mantis Boxing Hong Boxing, Shaolin Boxing, Bai He Boxing, and other boxing exercises, participated in boxing training classes and studied techniques of Western boxing, including the footwork, body movement, fist techniques and training methods from boxing documentary films of world champion Ted Lewis. He also specialized in the sticks, batons, nunchakus and other equipment and regularly took part in boxing matches; hence had very rich real life fighting experience. On one occasion, Bruce Lee fought against four knife-wielding thugs with bare hands in a Chinatown in Florida while rescuing a Chinese girl. Since then, Bruce Lee's name became widely known in the United States, and people started to pay more attention to Chinese Kung Fu.

1971年,李小龙回到香港,签约拍摄两部影片,第一部是预算只有10万美元的《唐山大兄》,影片创下香港电影最高票房纪录。第二部是《精武门》,李小龙在片中表现出的大无畏精神和惊人的打斗技巧,特别是"李三脚""地躺拳"和双节棍,令人赞不绝口,影片打破亚洲电影票房纪录。此后,李小龙成立协和电影公司,自编、自导、自演电影《猛龙过江》和《死亡游戏》,与美国好莱坞华纳电影公司联合拍摄《龙争虎斗》,并担任主角。

12 广东文化名人
Guangdong Celebrities

In 1971, Bruce returned to Hong Kong and was contracted to produce two films. The first one *The Big Boss* had only a US $ 100,000 budget, however, it broke the highest grossing revenues of Hong Kong film at that time. The second was *Fist of Fury*. Bruce Lee in the film showed the indomitable spirit and amazing fighting skills, in particular "Tripod", "Ground-Prone Boxing", and nunchakus, and the film received high praise from the public and also broke the Asian film box office records. Since then, Bruce Lee set up the Concorde Film Company where he wrote, directed, and starred in the movie *Way of the Dragon* and *Game of Death*, and jointly produced and starred in *Enter the Dragon* with Hollywood's Warner Brothers Film Company of the United States.

孙中山 Sun Yat-sen

孙中山（1866—1925）是广东省香山县（今中山市）人，名孙文，以"孙逸仙"闻名于世。

孙中山早年在檀香山、广州、香港等地求学。1897年到达日本，结识日本政府和民间各界人士，在旅日华侨中宣传革命，成立兴中会。1905年在日本东京领导成立中国同盟会，提出"民族、民权、民生"三民主义。1911年回到上海，被推选为"中华民国临时大总统"，并于1912年在南京宣誓就职，建立"中华民国临时政府"，组成临时参议院，颁布《中华民国临时约法》。1912年8月，同盟会改组为国民党。1924年，在广州召开中国国民党第一次全国代表大会，提出联俄、联共、扶助农工三大政策，把旧三民主义发展成为新三民主义，明确提出反帝纲领，促成第一次国共合作。后来创办黄埔军校，训练革命武装干部。1925年3月在北京逝世，1929年安葬于南京紫金山中山陵园。

12 广东文化名人
Guangdong Celebrities

Sun Zhongshan (1866-1925) was from Xiangshan County (now Zhongshan City), Guangdong Province, his formal name was Sun Wen, but he was widely known as Sun Yat-sen.

In his early years Sun Yat-sen studied in Honolulu, Guangzhou, Hong Kong and some other places. He arrived at Japan in 1897, became acquainted with the Japanese

government and local people from all sectors, propagated revolutionary thought among overseas Chinese, and established the Revive China Society. In 1905, the United League of China was established in Japan led by Sun Yat-sen, and he put forward Three Principles of the People, which are "Nationalism, Democracy and People's Livelihood". He went back to Shanghai in 1911, was elected as the provisional president of Republic of China, and sworn into office in 1912 in Nanjing, formed the Provisional Government and Interim Senate of the Republic of China, promulgated the Provisional Constitution of Republic of China. The United League of China was reorganized as the Kuomintang (KMT) in August 1912. The first National People's Congress of the Chinese Nationalist Party was held in Guangzhou in 1924, and proposed three main party policies, which were alliance with Russia, cooperation with Communist Party of China (CPC),and co-assistance to farmers and workers. He reformed old Three People's Principles to become the new Three People's Principles and specifically promoted anti-imperialism programme, which led to the realization of the first KMT-CPC cooperation. He then later founded the Whampoa Military Academy for training the Revolutionary Army cadres. He passed away in Beijing in March 1925 and buried in 1929 in Zhongshan Mausoleum, Zijinshan Mountain, Nanjing, Jiangsu Province.

孙中山组织革命政党，发动武装起义，领导了震惊中外的辛亥革命，推翻了中国历史上延续几千年的封建王朝专制统治，建立民国政府，开创了中国民主革命的新篇章。他全面地整合了近代西方资产阶级民主思想的重要成分，包括宪政民主，人民主权（选举、罢免、创制、复决），权力分立制衡，社会主义，等等。加上他个人认为有必要保留的中国传统制度机构——监察权与考试权，形成五权宪法学说。对西方现代思想在中国的普及起了巨大的推动作用。

孫文 公為下天 創侯先生疋

Sun Yat-sen formed the revolutionary party, launched an armed uprising, and led the 1911 Revolution, which shocked the world. The Revolution overthrew the feudal dynasty dictatorship lasting for thousands of years in Chinese history, established the government of the Republic, and opened a new chapter in China's democratic revolution. He comprehensively integrated important components of the modern Western bourgeois democratic ideas, including a constitutional democracy, the sovereignty of the people (election, dismissal, initiative, referendum), separation of powers, checks and balances, socialism, and so on. Together with those traditional Chinese system institutions, he personally believed, needed to retain, which were the rights to monitor and test, developed the doctrine of the five-power constitution. It greatly contributed to the promotion of the modern Western thinking in China.

冼星海 Xian Xinghai

冼星海（1905—1945）祖籍广东省番禺，出生在澳门一个船工家庭，是中国近代著名的作曲家、钢琴家，所作的曲中以《黄河大合唱》最为有名。

1928年，冼星海在上海国立音专学小提琴和钢琴。1929年到巴黎勤工俭学，师从著名提琴家帕尼·奥别多菲尔和作曲家保罗·杜卡。1931年考入巴黎音乐学院，在肖拉·康托鲁姆作曲班学习。1935年回国后，积极参加抗日救亡运动，创作了大量战斗性的群众歌曲。1938年任延安鲁迅艺术学院音乐系主任。后来，在教学之余创作了不朽名作《黄河大合唱》等作品。

冼星海共作歌曲数百首（现存250余首），大合唱4部、歌剧1部、交响曲2部、管弦乐组曲4部、狂想曲1部以及小提琴、钢琴等器乐独奏、重奏曲多首。《黄河大合唱》是冼星海最重要的代表作，影响也最大。作品创作于1939年3月，1941年在苏联重新整理加工而成。由诗人光未然作词，以黄河为背景，热情歌颂中华民族源远流长的光荣历史和中国人民坚强不屈的斗争精神，痛诉侵略者的残暴和人民遭受的深重灾难，展现了抗日战争的壮丽图景，并向全中国发出了民族解放的战斗号角，塑造了中华民族巨人般的英雄形象。

Xian Xinghai (1905-1945), native of Panyu District, Guangdong Province, was born in Macao in a seaman's family and was a well-known modern Chinese composer and pianist, most notable for the song "Yellow River".

In 1928, Xian Xinghai learned the violin and piano at the Shanghai National Music Institute. Then he went to Paris in 1929 for higher education self-supported by doing some part-time jobs, and studied under the famous viola player Jesper Austrian Duo Feier and composer Paul Dukas. In 1931, he was admitted to the Paris Institute of Music and studied music composition with Cholat Cantor Rum, a composer. After returning home in 1935, he actively participated in the Chinese people's resistance against Japan aggression and national salvation movement and created a large number of war songs. He took the position of dean of the Music Department of Yan'an Lu Xun Art Academy in 1938 of which during that period he created the immortal masterpiece" Yellow River "and other works in his pastime as a teacher.

Xian Xinghai wrote hundreds of songs (but only about 250 songs were found), 4 chorales, 1 opera, 2 symphonies, 4 orchestral suites, 1 rhapsody and many solos for violin, piano and other instruments. The "Yellow River" is the most important masterpiece of Xian Xinghai's life and it has an most important impact. It was composed in March 1939, and then revised in the Soviet Union in 1941. The works were worded by the poet Guang Weiran using the Yellow River as the theme, enthusiastically praised the glorious long history of the Chinese Nation and the Chinese People's indomitable fighting spirit, condemned brutal aggressors, and expressed the sufferings of Chinese people. It also showed the movement of the Chinese people's resistance against Japan aggression like a magnificent painting, and blew the battle horn for national liberation to the entire Chinese nation, thereby creating a great heroic image of the Chinese nation.

13 广东经济
Guangdong Economy

海上丝绸之路 Maritime Silk Road

丝绸之路，是古代中国与外国所有往来通道的统称。丝绸之路实际上并不是只有一条路，除了陆地上的丝绸之路以外，还有一条经过海路到达外国的路线，这就是海上丝绸之路。

3世纪30年代以来，广州一直都是海上丝绸之路的主要港口。唐宋时期，广州成为中国第一大港口，是世界闻名的东方港口城市，也是中国通往国外的出发地。由广州经南海、印度洋，到达波斯湾各个国家的航线，是当时世界上最长的远洋航线。元代时，福建泉州超过广州，成为中国的第一大港口，但广州仍然是中国的第二大港口。在海上丝绸之路的历史上，广州是唯一一个长盛不衰的港口。明清时期，以广州为起点的海上丝绸之路已经有3条航线；明初、清初，由于中国政府禁止外国人到中国沿海通商或中国人到海外经商，广州长时间处于一口通商的局面。1784年，美国"中国皇后"号访问广州，标志着美国直达广州的航线开通。

目前保存在广州市内各地的海上丝绸之路遗址共有20多处，其中包括南海神庙、光孝寺、莲花塔、沙面西式建筑等。

南宋时期古沉船"南海一号"的顺利出水，更加印证了广东海上丝绸之路的说法。

13 广东经济
Guangdong Economy

The Silk Road is the name for all the trade routes between China and foreign countries. It is actually not only one route, in addition to the well-known Silk Road on land there is also a route by sea to foreign lands. This is the Maritime Silk Road.

Since the 330's, Guangzhou has always been the major port of the Maritime Silk Road. During the Tang and Song Dynasties, Guangzhou became the largest port in China and the world-famous eastern port city of China to other countries. The route started from Guangzhou, by South China Sea and Indian Ocean, then arrived at the Persian Gulf countries and was the longest maritime trade route in the world. In the Yuan Dynasty, Quanzhou Port in Fujian Province overtook Guangzhou to become the largest port in China, but Guangzhou still remained the second largest. In the history of the Maritime Silk Road, Guangzhou is the only everlasting port. During the Ming and Qing Dynasties, originating from Guangzhou, there were three Maritime Silk Roads; in the early Ming and early Qing times, the Chinese government banned foreigners to trade along the Chinese coast or Chinese people to do business overseas. For a long time Guangzhou was the only port with an exception and in 1784, the "Empress of China", a ship from the United States, visited Guangzhou, which marked the opening of a direct trade route between China and the United States.

There are now more than 20 historical sites of the Maritime Silk Road around Guangzhou, including the Nanhai Temple (Temple of the South China Sea God), Guangxiao Temple, Lianhua (Lotus Flower) Tower and Shamian Western Architectures.

The successfully salvaged "Sunken Vessel Nanhai No. 1", the ancient trade ship of the Song Dynasty, proves the existence of Cantonese Maritime Silk Road.

改革开放 Reform and Opening-up

改革开放是20世纪70年代末中国开始实行的对内改革经济、对外开放的政策。

计划经济曾一度被认为是社会主义、共产主义的经济标志之一。自20世纪50年代以来,计划经济曾经为中国早期的经济恢复和初步发展做出了巨大贡献。但是,随着时间的推移,其弊端日渐明显。

安徽省凤阳县小岗村是中国农村改革的发源地。1979年,中国政府决定在深圳、珠海、厦门、汕头试办经济特区,福建省和广东省成为全国最早实行对外开放的省份之一。从1985年起,又陆续在长江三角洲、珠江三角洲、闽东南地区和环渤海地区开辟经济开放区。

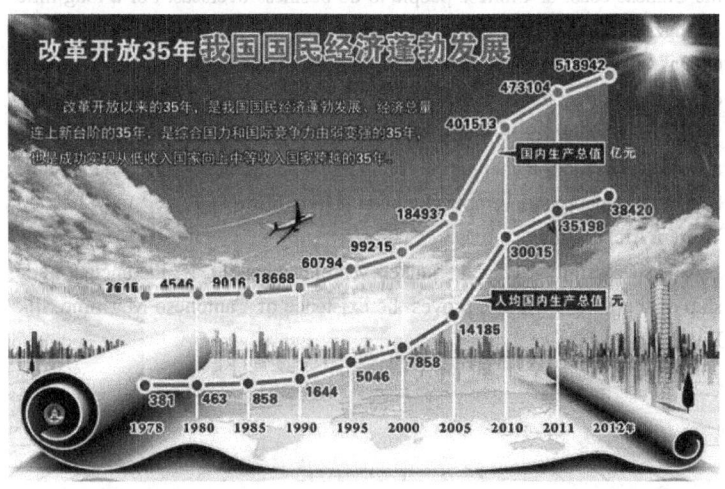

"Reform and opening-up" was the Chinese state policy in late 1970's that began to implement internal economic reform and "opening-up" of doors to the world.

Planned economy was once regarded as one of the socialist and communist economic symbols. In the 1950s, the planned economy contributed to China's early economic recovery and its initial development. However, over time, the drawbacks became apparent.

Xiaogang Village, Fengyang County in Anhui Province was the birthplace of China's rural reform. In 1979, the Chinese government decided to pilot special economic zones in Shenzhen, Zhuhai, Xiamen and Shantou areas; therefore Fujian and Guangdong Provinces became pioneers in the implementation of the opening-up policy. Since 1985, more economic zones have been established in the Yangtze River Delta, the Pearl River Delta, southeast Fujian and the Bohai Rim areas.

广东是中国经济第一强省,走在中国经济改革开放的前列。广东省在许多经济指标上列中国各省第一位,如地区生产总值、社会消费品零售总额、居民储蓄存款、专利申请量、税收、进出口总额、旅游总收入、移动电话拥有量、互联网用户总量、货物运输周转总量等。其中进出口总额年均占全国约1/4,从1985年至2008年连续23年居全国第一;累计吸引外商投资占全国约1/4;GDP从1989年至2010年连续21年居全国第一。广州市和深圳市是广东省经济最发达的城市。

广东以外向型经济为主,外商投资量大,对外经济仍以来料加工为主,受国际环境影响较大;主要集中于珠江三角洲地区,其中尤其以广州、深圳、佛山和东莞四市的经济总量最大;广东的制造业很发达,以陶瓷为主的建筑材料、以家具为主的居家装饰、以服装为主的轻纺产品一直主导中国内地市场。

在未来几年内,广东经济总量预计仍将居全国第一。

Guangdong Province has the largest economy of China, and is far ahead of others in adopting the policies of economic reform and opening-up. Many economic indicators of Guangdong Province are ranking first all of the Chinese provinces, such as Gross Domestic Product (GDP), total values of retail sales and consumer spending, household savings, number of patent applications, tax revenues, the volume of import and export trade, the total tourism revenues, number of mobile phone users, number of internet users and total tonnages of goods transport. Among the aforementioned, the average annual sum of imports and exports accounted for about a quarter of the national total, ranking number one in the country for 23 consecutive years from 1985 to 2008; Guangdong has also absorbed about a quarter of the total foreign investments of mainland China. The GDP has also ranked number one in the country for 21 consecutive years from 1989 to 2010. The cities of Guangzhou and Shenzhen in Guangdong Province are the most economically developed.

Guangdong's economy is export-based with a huge amount of foreign investment. The main businesses of manufacturing and processing still rely on external orders; therefore it is heavily impacted by the international economical environment. The manufacturing is mainly located in the Pearl River Delta region, specifically in the cities of Guangzhou, Shenzhen, Foshan and Dongguan. Manufacturing sectors of Guangdong are quite developed covering the areas of ceramic-based building materials, furniture and home decoration products, clothing and textile products dominating the mainland Chinese markets.

In the next few years, Guangdong's total economic output will most likely remain the nation's top ranking.

世界工厂 World's Factory

世界上每5台电脑就有一台是东莞制造,世界上每5件衬衫就有一件是在东莞生产的。诺基亚、雀巢、耐克、阿迪达斯、三星、金霸王、徐福记……这些世界知名品牌,都从东莞  这座功能强大的"世界工厂"走向世界各地。

1978年,东莞最早产生并形成了从事"来料加工""来样加工""来件装配"和"补偿贸易"的企业,称为"三来一补"。这种经济形式是改革开放初期中国内地创立的一种企业贸易形式。三十多年来,东莞所有的村镇几乎都发展成了专业从事某类产品加工制造的地方。东莞一时成为富甲一方的"广东四小虎"之一。

然而,作为"世界工厂"的东莞却没有创造出一个自己的世界知名品牌,在国际产业分工链条中只能处于最底层。更为严重的是,大量加工型企业源源不断地涌入东莞,使得东莞的土地、水、电资源与劳动力的矛盾日益突出。

如今的东莞市正在通过多种手段推动企业转型、经营转型、市场转型。从"东莞制造"到"东莞创造"虽然只有一字之差,但东莞要走的路却还很遥远。

One among every five computers in the world is "Made in Dongguan"; one of every five shirts in the world is also made in Dongguan. There are many worldwide and well-known brands, such as Nokia, Nestle, Nike, Adidas, Samsung, Duracell and Hsu Fu Chi, which go to the world market from Dongguan, so it is known as the "World's Factory".

In 1978, Dongguan gradually started manufacturing models of "manufacturing with supplied materials", "manufacturing with supplied samples and design", "assembling with supplied parts" and "compensation trade", known as "Three-supplied and one compensation". This form of economy was a kind of trade model developed by mainland China in the early stage of economy reform and opening-up. For over thirty years, almost all of the towns and villages in Dongguan have become specialized in manufacturing one of these products. Dongguan then became one of the "Four Little Tigers in Guangdong", a very rich area.

However, as the "World's Factory", Dongguan did not create a single world-class brand of its own; therefore the city could only remain at the very bottom of international supply chain. At the same time, a large number of manufacturing companies also came to Dongguan, which created great shortages of land, water and power resources in addition to a lack of labour resources.

Nowadays, Dongguan is trying to promote "corporate restructuring", "business transformation" and "market evolution" with the aim of converting the term, "Made in Dongguan" to "Created in Dongguan". There is only one word difference, but there is a long journey to go.

广交会 Canton Fair

广交会,全称为中国进出口商品交易会。创办于1957年春季,是中国目前历史最长、层次最高、规模最大、商品种类最全、到会客商最多、成交效果最好的综合性国际贸易盛会。

广交会由几十个交易团组成,有几千家外贸公司、生产企业、科研院所、外商投资或独资企业、私营企业参展。除传统的看样成交外,还举办网上交易会。以出口贸易为主,也涵盖进口贸易,还开展多种形式的经济技术合作与交流以及商检、保险、运输、广告、咨询等业务活动。

每年春秋两季广交会在广东省广州市海珠区阅江中路382号琶洲国际会展中心举办。春季开展时间为每年4月15日至5月5日,秋季开展时间为每年10月15日至11月4日。广交会分三期举行,每期都有不同的参展范围。第一期包括大型机械及设备、小型机械、自行车、摩托车、汽车配件、化工产品、五金、工具、车辆、家用电器、电子电气产品、照明产品、建筑及装饰材料等。第二期包括餐厨用具、日用陶瓷、工艺陶瓷、家居装饰品、玻璃工艺品、家具、编织及藤铁工艺品、园林产品、铁石制品、家居用品、个人护理用品、浴室用品、钟表眼镜、玩具、礼品及赠品、节日用品、土特产品等。第三期包括服装、食品、医药及保健品、医疗器械、体育及旅游休闲用品、办公文具、鞋、箱包等。

Canton Fair, full namely the China Import and Export Commodities Fair, was founded in the spring of 1957. It is now a comprehensive international trade event in China with the longest history, the highest quality, the largest scale, most variety of goods, most number of businessmen and largest turnover.

Canton Trade Fair consists of dozens of trading groups, participated in by thousands of foreign trade companies, manufacturing enterprises, research institutes, sole foreign investment or owned enterprises and other private sectors. In addition to the traditional ways of viewing and ordering, internet online trade fairs are also organized. The main business is not only to export, but also to provide business of import trade.There are also all sorts of economic and technological cooperation and exchanges, commodity inspections, insurance, transportation, advertising, consulting and other service business activities.

The event takes place twice every year during the spring and autumn seasons and is held at the Pazhou International Exhibition Centre, 382 Yuejiang Zhonglu, Guangzhou City, Guangdong Province. The Spring Fair opens between April 15th and May 5th , with the Autumn Fair between October 15th and November 4th every year. There are three phases in each fair and each phase has a different product theme. The first one is for large-scale machinery and equipment, small machinery, bicycles, motorcycles, automobile parts, chemical products, hardware, tools, vehicles, household appliances, electronic and electrical products, lighting products, construction and decoration materials,etc. The second phase includes kitchen utensils, household ceramics, industrial ceramics, home accessories, glass crafts, furniture, weaving and rattan crafts, garden products, metal and stone products, household goods, personal care appliances, toiletries, watches, glasses, toys, gifts, souvenirs, tourist products, local products, etc. The third phase includes clothing, food, medicine and health products, medical equipment, sports, travel and leisure products, office stationery, shoes, bags, etc.